It Is Done!

Dr. Izdihar Jamil, Ph.D.

15 Secrets to Manifest Your Dream Life from Inspiring Entrepreneurs Around the World

Publishing History

Edition 1 / February 2021
ISBN: 9798702180458
Imprint: Independently Published

Dedications

A big thank you to my husband, family, and friends for your love and support. Thank you to my best friend who's always cheering for me. Thank you to my coaches and clients for your love and trust. Thank you Mama and Ayah for your love, and I hope I make you proud. To all that have a big vision – this book is for you.

Ba and Nada, Mommy loves you very much!

Kind regards,

~ Dr. Izdihar Jamil

I want to thank Danielle Peralta, my best friend and future wife, for her support and strength as I go through this unbelievable journey.

I also want to thank my parents and brother for their support and unconditional love.

Lastly, I want to thank Dr. Izdihar Jamil for the opportunity to be featured in this powerful book alongside these amazing entrepreneurs.

~ Christian Rey Perez

To everyone who supported my writing and believed in me long before I was able to take ownership and believe in myself. I cherish each of you for your encouragement and thank you from the bottom of my heart.

~ Deb Rosman

To my beloved family members, especially Along Nisaa and Aimy who had made this chapter possible for me, and everyone else who had been contributing the puzzle pieces to complete my life. Thank you so much for always being there for me.

~ Hany Hanana

I need to take a quick moment and thank my incredible husband, Tyler, for being the man of strength and compassion that he is, and for always believing in me and my dreams. To my many coaches and mentors in my life that have been a support, a sounding board, insisting on accountability, and holding unwavering faith – I am forever grateful!

Thank you!

~ Jessica Fox

Dedications

I dedicate my chapter to my true driving purpose, Lola and Val.
~ **Matt Baruning**

I would like to take this opportunity to thank my mother, Janet Trevor, who has always been my rock and from whom I get my strength of never giving up, and also, my beautiful children. Dominica teaches me to be assertive, bold, and caring. Ella teaches me to be vivacious, creative, and fun. Matthias teaches me to be just me, unique and special in my own quirkiness.
~ **Michelle Jones**

I'd like to dedicate this chapter to my parents and my children. My parents are my inspiration and I love them dearly. I am the resilient and focused woman that I am today because of their sacrifices. To my children, you have grounded and stretched me in ways I never imagined. You are four of the BRIGHTEST stars in the multiverse, full of unlimited potential and the ability to live whatever life you want. Decide that you want the best, align your energy, claim and manifest it!
~ **Naomi Beverely**

I want to thank my husband, Amir Esa, and my son for being with me during those trying moments when I was at my lowest points. Your support, encouragement, and dedication in helping me get back on my feet is greatly appreciated and loved.
~ **Nor Suhir**

I want to thank the universe for all the lessons learnt and my parents who have always taught me to believe in myself and follow my heart. Last but not the least, I would like to extend my gratitude to Izdihar Jamil and Jessica Fox for giving me this opportunity and to all the readers who would flip the pages of my chapter.
~ **Priyanka Mukherjee**

I want to thank my children, Sakeena, Yusef, and Suraya. You have been my inspiration. Thank you for always shining beauty and love into my life.
~ **Razia Naqvi-Jukes**

Dedications

To my children: Jaydee, Hyrum, Talon and Quinten.... May you have the courage to follow your dreams.

~ **Vandee Flake**

Thank you, my friends, family, and mentors who played an enormous part in my growth and success; for guiding me to uncover the genuine gold within and deeper self-awareness and love. You know who you are. Thank you Mother/Father/God for connection and the truth about who I really am and how much I have to offer.

~ **Veronica Crystal Young**

Thank you to all who supported me in making this book possible. Special thanks to Mark Joseph, Kristin Taylor, Hilary Broadbent, and Michelle Mehta for their feedback and for editing my work. I dedicated this book to my loving mother and my inspiration, Francisca Angkiangco (transitioned 2019).

~ **Veronica Joseph**

Book Reviews

Dr. Izdihar Jamil is an inspiration. Her story of getting herself into the media is not only empowering, it's impactful. Her knowledge and experience is high class and she delivers her story in a fun and inspiring way. We can all learn something from Izdihar.

Do what she says and your dreams of becoming a world class and well known leader in your industry will come true.

~ **Melissa Desveaux**, Author and Author Consultant, Australia

What a powerful read!

In her chapter of *It Is Done,* **Izdihar Jamil** highlights her successful method around who you are choosing to be, how you think, what you feel, and the actions you take are the first steps to creating your desired life. An absolute MUST-read.

~ **Ingrid Saenger**, Health and Fitness Coach, USA

Wise, impactful and inspiring read. Highly recommended for aspiring entrepreneurs!

~ **Dr. Tasnuva Tunna,** Autism Health Coach, Canada

What a powerful testament of exploring one's fullest potential! Regardless of your background or start in life, you can do it!! Check out this inspiring read!

~ **Jessie Sawyers**, Founder and CEO of Getting Unlocked, USA

Great ideas to expand your network!! I am new to word-of mouth marketing, and this chapter gave me some next level tips and ideas. I am inspired to make my first *TikTok*, too!

~ **Sean McCreary**, Author and Graphic Designer, USA

I'll put these word-of-mouth marketing tips to use! I plan to expand my business over the next few years. This chapter has given me some ideas on how to build a strong foundation. Great read!

~ **James McCreary**, Entrepreneur and Web Developer, USA

I am excited to make use of these ideas! I am getting ready to publish my first book this year. I will use all of these skills I learned to use word-of-mouth marketing with my own project! Well done!

~ **Seana Beverly**, Aspiring Author, USA

If you're looking for a story about transforming trauma into triumph and fear into hope with the law of attraction, look no further. The stories **Deb Rosman** shares will help you learn how to not let fear run your life but instead how to turn fear into positivity with the power of law of attraction.

~ **Abby Norman**, Leadership Expert & Executive Coach, abbyleadershipcoaching.com

Just now finished reading it..., emotional tears in my eyes..., beautiful encouraging an touchy..., and especially something any woman can relate to herself. Love the end with the caterpillar quote! The beginning quote too is awesome regarding the journey. I'm sooooo proud of you..., commendable..., love it absolutely!

~ **Anu**

It's written straight from the heart. I enjoyed reading it.

~ **Yasmin Srikanth, Admin Manager**

The read is very interesting, moving, and motivating for thought leaders!

~ **Michelle Mehta**, Teen Confidence Expert, USA

Dr. Joseph writes straight from the heart about the inspiring journey that brought her to practice Chinese medicine, and the principles of openness and compassion that guide her success.

~ **Dr. Hilary Broadbent**, Doctor of Oriental Medicine, USA

Three cheers for **Veronica** whose words are wise, powerful, and inspiring!

~ **Kristin Clark Taylor, author, USA**

Powerful, Captivating, and Overflowing with Wisdom and will profoundly impact anyone who has experienced a painful past. **Veronica Crystal Young** is an extremely talented writer who beautifully and transparently shares her story and will inspire any reader to have the courage and be empowered on their journey to healing.

~ **Jen Coffel**, CEO Engaging Speakers Inc, United States

After reading **Priyanka**'s chapter I felt inspired and elated, and most of all, I felt a sense truth as if she was walking in my shoes! I felt privileged to be able to share this part of her journey, and that's what it felt like, as if I was there with her! This chapter was heartfelt, honest, and refreshing and very true and raw, yet written with compassion for the self.

Thank you, **Priyanka**, for sharing your thoughts, your feelings, and your emotions and experiences to inspire the next generation to walk their path in truth and honesty and become the best version of themselves.

~ **Phil Smith, England**

Priyanka's debut book is a powerful message to everyone out there who feel lost and lack motivation in life as well as to people who simply want to achieve those much-desired goals.

In her chapter, aptly titled 'Life is all about choices', **Priyanka** uses her personal experiences to show readers that even when all seem lost and there doesn't appear to be any glimmer of hope, we can still take charge of your lives and turn things around. Not just empty words, she includes clear steps and action plan which will help readers understand and embrace the amazing power of Law of Attraction.

In challenging times that we live in where we all are rushing with our lives moving from one task to the next, we often forget the most important thing – loving ourselves, and this is exactly what **Priyanka** reminds us very powerfully in this chapter. 'Self-love is not selfish; you cannot truly love another until you know how to love yourself'.

The simple, clear and concise way **Priyanka** explains the concept of the Law of Attraction and practical steps on how we could manifest the kind of life we want would be hugely beneficial to readers. This is a how-to-change-your-life handbook!
~ **Sanhati Sinha Roy, England**

It's never too late to become a better you, a happier you. This is exactly what **Priyanka** lays out before you. A way to change and reshape your life to become the best version of you. With her positive and inspirational words, she shows you how to achieve the life you want just like she has succeeded in accomplishing hers. This journey is all about looking inwards and changing who you are, as you only get back from the universe what you project out to others. And **Priyanka** is here to help
~ **Kris Mcdivitt, Scotland**

An inspiring story for entrepreneurs, as well as anyone recovering from a stroke or a sudden diagnosed debilitating disease.
~ **Nieves M. Pinero**, Entrepreneur, USA

A great fighter in body and soul! A very strong-in-spirit-type of person who has gone through real tragic life experiences herself. Through her strength and desire to go on, she never fails to inspire others who have also gone through the ups and downs of life, and to be able to stand up against all odds and move on once again! Thanks **Nor**!
~ **Diana Yap**, D'Cusines Restaurant and Catering, Singapore

A must-read for young entrepreneurs to learn from this wise guru.
~ **Shahrul & Shida**, Wizworld Management (M) Sdn Bhd, Malaysia

This is a unique collection of unfettered thinking and straightforward advice. There are words of wisdom here for everyone.
~ **John Avenell**, Businessman, Australia

Makes me want to be 'Konmari-ed' myself and achieve greater things!~ **Nisaa**, Mom and Wife, Malaysia

Very raw and inspiring. It provides the reader an opportunity to embark on a new avenue for success. It is a remarkable story of Vandee's own life's struggles turned into victory. It also teaches how to develop a positive mindset, choosing the right people to connect with, and how commitment and consistency in everything that we do in life or in business are what matters most. It's a simple but powerful read for all to find a way to win in life, which the world needs.

~ **Kai Hayes**, Author of *Lion at Heart: Discovering Courage and Greatness Within*, a Leadership, Personal and Spiritual Growth book, and a Global Business Owner and Mentor, USA

Wow! She nailed it! I love how she engaged with the reader's feelings, shared personal experiences, and made it so real! I feel like I can do this! And so inspired to run harder! And be the better version of myself.

~ **Anna Merrill**, Illustrator and Entrepreneur, USA

Spot on! Gratitude, Goals/Vision, Positive Social Circle, and Action is needed to achieve any success. Thanks for sharing!

~ **Lee Vugrenes**, Author of *All Things for Your Own Good: An Illegitimate Orphan Korean Boy's Keys to Happiness*, USA

Inspiring indeed!

~ **Carolyn Street**, Author, Singapore

Table of Contents

Foreword

In this "How-To" book for entrepreneurs, Dr. Izdihar Jamil, Ph.D., lays out the "secrets" to being successful. Some of these ideas could be things you have heard before; others may even seem far-fetched to you at this moment. All of them deserve to be given a second thought and perhaps reconsidered.

In her own successful journey to make her dreams a reality, Dr. Jamil has sought the wisdom of some of the best thinkers and most successful people across a vast array of disciplines. In these pages, she reveals what those people have reported as the key principles at work in their own lives, as well as the methods used to put those tools to good use.

She has done the research and collaborated with other entrepreneurs to give you the business foundation required to be on the right trajectory. What remains for you is only to absorb and incorporate this knowledge and draw upon the magic inherent in these powerful concepts. Set something in motion. Put an idea into practice. Be watchful and allow the process to work in tandem with you. Let the success that you see for yourself come into being, and then pass it on as the author has done.

My last word for you would be to follow your heart. It has served me well in my years of business.

Robert Goldberg
Co-Founder – Earth Island
https://followyourheart.com

Introduction

Hey Love!

I'm Vanessa. I was sexually abused by multiple men as a small child. I was homeless at 16. My five-year-old son died of cancer. My home got totally flattened by an overturned tanker while I was out shopping and eight months pregnant, and I became homeless again.

I've been bankrupt, lost my sight, ability to walk, and was having seizures daily. I was told I would be fully disabled by experts. Despite all of that, I LIVE AN AMAZING LIFE!

I have six beautiful children and have the best relationship ever with an amazing guy who fully supports my work. A few years ago, I enabled him to retire, and now he has the freedom to focus on his passion.

I make millions online. I have fully healed my seizures, and I can walk and see again. I live in multi-million homes around the world.

I love to help women to make lots of money, heal, and live abundant lives. I'm the real deal to teach it. I also work high-end with celebs, multi-millionaires, and people that you would know!

Introduction

Despite my challenges, I am living the life that I desired in both family and business. How is it possible? By releasing my blocks, following a proven system, and consistently take action. No matter where you are, you have the power to create your life. You have to allow yourself to experience your success and money. I believe in keeping things simple and believe that things are easy, and so… It Is Done!

The entrepreneurs in this book have experienced challenges in their lives and, more importantly, overcome them. They are showing you the steps that you can model to create the life that you desired. These are real people with real results. By following their footsteps, you have a great tool to create the life that you desire.

Here's to celebrating your success!

Vanessa Ogden Moss xx
7-Figure Entrepreneur
Featured in *Forbes* and on *FOX TV*

It Is Done!

Dr. Izdihar Jamil, Ph.D.

"For things to change, I must change FIRST."
~ Dr. Izdihar Jamil, Ph.D.

Quantum Leap Creation

Dr. Izdihar Jamil, Ph.D.
Business Coach, USA

"For things to change, I must change FIRST."
~ Dr. Izdihar Jamil, Ph.D.

I was crushed! *"You're not famous enough to be in the media!"* someone once told me. I was crushed. I felt really sad and worthless to be put down like that. Sure, I'm not a member of the world-famous Kardashians or as controversial as Lady Gaga, but I do have my own unique story and have overcome indescribable challenges to get where I am today.

In my reflection, I asked myself, *"Why am I so upset? What is the truth from my perspective?"* More importantly, I questioned myself as to *"Why do I care so much about what that person says? Why am I giving my power over to them?"*

At that moment, I chose to let go of all those disempowering beliefs. I chose to bring the power back to me and shift the focus back to me. I believe that I have a beautiful message to share with the world. I believe that other people have ZERO power over me.

I chose to stand in my power and have faith that God is my sole Provider and that He will bless me for what is rightfully mine. For things to change, I must change first. It isn't about them; it's about me. For me to create the life that I desire, it has to start with me.

Soon, I had success beyond my wildest imagination. I was featured on *Forbes*, one of the most iconic brands in the world, sharing how to build brand authority in a brand-new niche so that it's in alignment with my *Forbes* feature. I got into *TED-Ed*, one of the most prestigious speaking platforms in the world, sharing my story about the Power of Rejection. I appeared on *FOX TV,* sharing my secrets on how entrepreneurs can make money without any paid advertising.

I was featured on hundreds of influential media such as *NBC*, *ABC*, *CBS*, *Business Innovator*, *Thrive Global*, and many others. I got featured on

1

the front cover of *The Corporate Escapist Magazine* and had an expert feature in *W G Magazine*. I am constantly being invited to speak on high-profile speaking platforms and podcasting shows.

As a result, it has helped me tremendously grow my business. I attracted and secured amazing clients from all around the world. My association with these powerful and influential brands has helped me position myself in the Top 1% of authorities in my field. I instantly have the credibility as an expert through endorsements from those brands. So, when I meet my clients, my brand does most of the selling for me. All I focus on is figuring out the best way to help my clients.

The truth is, I didn't know that all that would be possible, but I had a vision and methods that helped me to create all those incredible results. I'll be sharing those in this chapter, so make sure you continue reading because success is your destiny!

Have you got someone who has told you that you can't do something before?

This is my story, and I hope it'll inspire you to keep moving forward because one day, your dreams will become a reality. It's inevitable...

It Is Done!

The Humble Beginning

I grew up in Malaysia and then moved to England after getting married to be with my husband. In England, I worked and was awarded Ph.D. in Computer Science. While doing my Ph.D., my husband and I started an organic delivery company that delivers organic produce from the farm to the customers' doors.

I was pregnant with my first child and wanted to create a healthy food choice. At the same time, my husband and I were also intrigued by the idea of financial freedom and wanted to create a business so that we could achieve financial freedom. We combined our need in creating a healthy living with a need to service the community to create our own organic delivery business. A business is about solving peoples' problems, and that's exactly what we did.

I took that opportunity to practice many business fundamentals that I learned. The best way to learn is to do it in real life and not just reading books or going to seminars. I learned how to get clients without any paid advertising, which I still do today. Of course, I've gotten better over the years too. ☺

I learned about marketing, sales, product development, building a team and a system, and many other things. What I want to share is building a business takes time, and it's not something instant. You have to exercise the muscle. So if you want to shift your career to entrepreneurship, my #1 advice would be to create a part-time business while doing your existing job. Not only will you have security in place without worrying about money coming in, but you'll also get to have the time that you need to practice various aspects of the business.

In other words, don't do anything drastic, like suddenly diving 30 days' notice to start your business. I have never seen anyone make money in their business within 30 days of leaving their job, especially for newbies. It took me over 10 years of an entrepreneurship journey to get me where I am today.

Now, I'm not saying that you need 10 years to establish a business. What I'm saying is that you need to give yourself permission to be successful by giving yourself the time to learn all the business fundamentals. You can't build a business without a solid foundation. It'll crumble in the first stiff wind blow. A strong business foundation will allow your business not only to survive but also thrive in the test of time and changing economic situations.

The Move

From England, we moved to America in 2015 so that my husband could have his dream job. I left my secured job position and closed down our organic delivery business for a new start in America. However, our life here wasn't the picture-perfect one that we imagined. We were faced with horrible social abuse that led me to have one of the worst times in my life.

The irony is that during those dark times, I felt that God was giving me a sign to start my coaching and consultancy business. It's not just my way of healing from the challenges but also a way for me to help others because I always believed that I was meant for something great.

If you want to find out more about my challenges and how I used that to start my online business, you can read it in my #1 International Bestselling Book *13 Key Strategies to Make Money Fast In Business* available here:

https://www.amazon.com/dp/1697242979

The Challenge

I first started to teach moms how to save money with consistency and predictability. It was something that I had the skills for and also because I knew moms had a tough time saving money due to the high expense of running a family. One of my great friends was my first client, and she gave me the confidence to move forward.

I'm really thankful that I have amazing people supporting me in my journey towards success. That's one of my secrets to success — you've got to have amazing people supporting you because there's no way you can do it on your own.

From there, I moved on to teach other female entrepreneurs how to attract clients and make sales. However, my biggest challenge then was solidifying my credibility as an expert. I was a computer scientist turned entrepreneur. I had to start from scratch. So why would potential clients choose me over more established experts? I found that I was constantly being compared to others, and more of then than not, I was not the one they chose to work with.

I had to work really, really, really hard to convince people that I'm really good at what I do. Then, when it comes to my actual skills, I was exhausted because I've spent my energy convincing people that I'm good at what I do. At times I felt helpless because I felt that I couldn't compete with the big names in the industry.

The Turning Point

One day, I was invited to be part of a book project called *She Made it Happen*. I shared my entrepreneurship story, and the book hit #1 in multiple countries. Instantly, I was seen as an expert because of the success of my book. You can ready about my story in *She Made it Happen* here:

http://www.lulu.com/content/paperback-book/she-made-it-happen/26046439

I used my #1 Bestseller book as an asset to propel my business, including:

- As a lead magnet to attract quality clients;

- As a pitching tool to get into the media;

- As a tool to get the attention of high profile editors and journalists at *Forbes, Entrepreneurs, Business Insider,* etc.;

- Connecting with high profile influencers;

- Getting into prestigious speaking platforms and podcasting interviews;

- As another source of income by helping other entrepreneurs to be a bestselling author.

Suddenly, things started to shift. People are now reaching out to me because I'm a well-known expert as endorsed by the media and other influential brands. I didn't have to prove myself anymore because my brand does all the selling for me. I am seen as a trusted authority in my field, which means I can focus more on using my skill set to help others.

Now, I feel really blessed to be able to help many female entrepreneurs become the top authority in their field using various media platforms while wildly growing their business. If you want to find out more about what I do, I offer a FREE 1-day course called "The Fast Authority Accelerator" that you can check out here: https://www.izdiharjamil.com/fast-authority

The Creation – Lessons and Wisdom

How was I able to create such success in the shortest time possible? The law of physics states that everything is energy. Thoughts, feelings, actions, materials, etc., have a form of energy vibration. So, if everything is energy, including my thoughts, I might as well choose my thoughts, dreams, goals, and desires, right?

That's exactly what I did because what you focus on expands, so I chose to focus on the things that really matter to me. Here are the five ways that I use to create my life. I may use one, some, or all of them, but each one has laid the foundation of the results in my life.

When they are combined, it's just explosive!

#1 Visualization

I would visualize how I want to have things in my mind. It's like playing a movie in your head. There's a scene, the colors, the people, the feeling, the conversation, etc. Just let your mind wander. You're basically planting a seed in your head. The beauty of it is that your mind can't differentiate between reality and a made-up world. It just thinks they are the same. So, if you feel like it, see it happening, and everything is played out in your mind, what are the chances of it truly happening? Very, very likely.

For example, in my #1 International Bestselling Book *Yes I Can! 22 Success Secrets of Inspiring People Around the World*, I shared how my Ph.D. paper publication was rejected for six years. Somehow, I had a vision of myself speaking on an international stage because my work was accepted and recognized at a prestigious publication. One day I got the email saying YES!, that my work was accepted, and there I was speaking on an international stage exactly how I envisioned it.

You can check out my book here to read more about I overcome my challenges: https://www.amazon.com/dp/B0858TTVQ2

You can also see my presentation on the international stage in front of the top people in the industry here:

https://www.youtube.com/watch?v=y7jCr6RNXNk

#2 Prayer

Since I was a little girl, I always thought to ask God for help. There's only so much a human being can do, and the rest is up to the Creator. Do you know when there are times, and you've done everything that you could have done and yet nothing happened or when you feel like you've been pushed into a corner and there is no way out? That's the moment when I would bow in prostration and ask God for help. Let go and give it up to God.

I would pray something like,

> "God, my Helper, the Most Merciful, the Giver of All. I'm weak. Lift this burden off me. Show me the lessons that I need to learn from this and make it good. Help me to make this happen in my life if it is good for me. If it is not good for me, take it away and replace it with something better. Bring good people in my life that can help me. Help me, my Creator, because there's no one else who can help me. Help me so that I can help others and take care of my family. Help me to make it happen because you're the one with all the Power. Unto you, I surrender".

For example, I have always wanted to be featured on *Forbes*, one of the most iconic, prestigious, and globally recognized brands in the world. I've built a relationship with a top *Forbes* journalist for almost a year. I'm doing the actions that I need to do to take me a step closer. But I still wasn't on *Forbes*. What was missing?

So, almost everyday, when I prostrate in humility to my Creator in my prayers, I would say *"God, The Giver of All, please help me to be featured on* Forbes *by 31 December so that I can help others"*. I pretty much said the same thing for a year.

Then one day, some time at the end of November, I was speaking to a very successful entrepreneur who is a multi-seven-figure earner and has been featured on *Forbes* multiple times. She said that *Forbes* is looking for someone like me because I'm rare – a Muslim woman who's out there and having a successful online business. I said, "YES! Let's do it!" …and together, we made it happen. It turned out the relationship that I built with the *Forbes* writer for almost a year, and all my consistent actions have turned into a golden fruit.

Check out my article in *Forbes* here where I share how to position yourself as the top authority in your field and attract high-quality clients:

http://bit.ly/3bwN8xH

You can also search "Izdihar Jamil Forbes" on *Google* and the article will come up.

The cool part of this is that now I'm able to teach women how to do it too. You can check out my FREE 1-day course, "The Fast Authority Accelerator," to find out more about being featured in high-profile media here:

https://www.izdiharjamil.com/fast-authority

#3 Declaration

I was on *Facebook* when I saw someone who was featured on TV shared their pictures. I said to myself, *I would love to be on TV too!* I saw it in my mind happening, and I prayed for it to happen. When I say "declaration," I mean to verbally declare it out to the world. There's something special about declaring it because your words create your world. It's like you making an announcement to the world.

As I go on with my work, I help someone to get a good client. As a thank you, that amazing person offered me the opportunity to be featured on *FOX TV*. I was EXCITED because my declaration came true. So verbally declare your intentions and then take action. Sometimes the actions that you take don't have to be directly connected with your goals, but you do need to take some form of action to set the momentum up.

You can check out my interview on *FOX TV* where I share the solutions to help entrepreneurs make more sales in their business without paid advertising here:

https://www.fox4now.com/the-morning-blend/female-leaders-spotlight-with-izdihar

#4 Write it Down

There's something magical when you see things in black and white. It's like the law has been laid out. If you noticed that all the laws are written down as part of the constitution. As a result, every single citizen in that country has to obey the law because it is written down. This book is written down. It's like documenting history or a future that is for sure happening. That's why people write things down because it's part of a law of creation.

For example, I wanted to be featured on *TED-Ed*, one of the most prestigious speaking platforms in the world. The top leaders and highly influential people have been featured on *TED-Ed*, but I didn't know how to bo about doing that.

So, almost every day, I would write an email to myself about my goals. One of them is to be featured on *TED-Ed,* and I included a timeline for it.

Always include a timeline. That's the difference between a dream and a goal. I said something like, "I am featured on *TED-Ed* by 31 December this year." You can choose to write it on *Google* docs, a journal, notes on your phone, or any other methods that you choose. I choose to write an email to myself as that fits my lifestyle better. The key here is just to write it down.

One day, the right people and knowledge came to me, and I was featured on *TED-Ed*! Sometimes I still pinch myself whether it's real. You can check out my presentation here on "Turning Fear Into Success":

https://ed.ted.com/on/3CGIJgOg

I would use the same method of writing down my ideal clients to help me attract the right clients to my business and my life, too. Give it a go. Write down your goals consistently. If you can't do it every day, you can do it on a weekly basis to set up the momentum.

If you're interested, you can check out my Guided five-minute goal-setting journal to help you hit your goals with ease here:

https://www.amazon.com/Yes-Can-Setting-Journal-Accomplish/dp/B08R9YH29Q

#5 Action

If meditation and the Law of Attraction can solve all problems, we would all be rich and happy by now. The truth is, the Law of Attraction and meditation are not enough because they are operating on the inner world or the unseen. Results happen in the physical world. So, what's the bridge between the inner world and the physical world?

It's ACTION. Action is the bridge between the inner world and the physical world. Action produces results.

For example, I wanted to speak on this high-profile podcast. It's one of the top podcasts on *Apple iTunes*. So, I approached the podcast host and asked if I could appear in his podcast. He said, "Maybe..."

So, I created an event with the host. At the end of the event, I told him, "I'm setting the intention to be on your podcast next year!"

He said. "Sure you can, Izzy! I've sent you a private link on how you can be in the show".

OMG! It is DONE! darlings!

So, take action, as it is the bridge to your success in the physical world.

I'm saying YES to...

I feel really thankful that I've been blessed with these amazing opportunities. Not only that, but I have been able to help women be successful and make more money in their businesses. I have also been able to create a better life for my family.

So for the next three years, I'm saying YES! to:

- Helping 3,000 women to be the be in the top 1% of the authorities in their field;

- Creating an exclusive retreat to help entrepreneurs write their book in 48 hours at one of the most beautiful private islands in the world;

- Helping hundreds of entrepreneurs get high-profile media (*Forbes, Entrepreneur Magazine*, TV) and speaking gigs;

- Automating my business fully so I can make $50K a month with ease WITHOUT having to do any sales calls;
- Having a highly-skilled team and a profitable system so I can walk away at any moment;
- Creating a profitable retirement for my family and me;
- Living my best possible life surrounded by people that I love and trust the most.

Remember, your word is LAW. In this chapter, you have the tools that you need to create the life that you desire. The question is only how bad do you want it? Are you willing to do whatever it takes to make it happen, or are you just going to give up?

You are a POWERFUL creator, and you are meant for GREATNESS in this world. So, choose every moment to live in your power, and you will see your life changing and growing more than in your wildest imagination.

Power Summary

Let's recap some of the key ideas in this book:

1. What's one method that I use as part of my creation?
2. What is the bridge between the inner world and the physical world?
3. What is the first step that I used to build my credibility?

Key Actions

Actions produce results. So here are three actions that can help you move closer to your goals:

1. Write down three goals that you have. Remember to include a timeline in it. You can use the *5-Minute Goal-Setting Journal* that I've created here to do that:

   https://www.amazon.com/Yes-Can-Setting-Journal-Accomplish/dp/B08R9YH29Q

2. What is one simple action that you can do today to help you move closer to your goals?

3. Fill in the blanks. I _____ [have, earn, make am] _____ [your goals] by _____ [date]. For example I am featured on *Entrepreneur.com* by 31st Dec 2021.

"Your success is inevitable. Just keep moving forward every day and trust that It Is Done!, and so it IS!"
~ Dr. Izdihar Jamil

Love and blessings,

Izdihar xx

About the Author

Dr. Izdihar Jamil, Ph.D., is a multiple #1 International Bestselling Author and *TED-Ed* presenter. She was featured on *Forbes*, *FOX TV,* and major publications such as *NBC*, *ABC*, *Business Innovator,* and *Thrive Global*.

In September 2020, she was chosen to be on the front cover of *The Corporate Escapist Magazine* because of her inspirational story.

She loves helping women be in the Top 1% of authorities in their field by helping them be bestselling authors, getting them booked in the media, for speaking gigs,TV, magazines, and on *TED-Ed.*

It is her greatest pleasure to see women having confidence in themselves and be successful in their business so they can take care of their families. Her methods are proven, simple, and effective – designed to produce the fastest results possible for her clients.

In her spare time, she loves baking and reading.

Contacts

Website: www.izdiharjamil.com

Social media: @izdiharjamil

Bestselling Books: https://www.amazon.com/dp/B08DBHD4HX

FREE Gift: FREE course "The Fast Authority Accelerator"
- How to book speaking gigs, media *(Forbes, Entrepreneur, Business Insider)*, and *TED-Ed.*

https://www.izdiharjamil.com/fast-authority

10 Lessons of High Performers

Christian Rey Perez
Masters of Life Podcast, Las Vegas, NV

*"How can I leave my mark on the world, I thought, unless I
get out there first and see it.."*
~ Phil Knight, Nike Founder

I'm not good at names."

I've said this too many times to too many people. Anyone else?

I used to think that there is no way I could remember the name of every person I met, but I hate to break it to you, the truth is... **Wait!**

Before we get into that, I'd like you to know my story.

*   *   *

I came from a middle-class family with insane-level dreams of being rich. In high school, I knew I wanted to be in business or corporate America. I knew what it took to get there. I loved public speaking, I loved sales, and I loved people. I worked hard in high school, got into college, and took business courses. During college, I got an internship at Enterprise Rent-A-Car, which has a well-respected sales and management program.

Yes, I was just as shocked as you are.

During my time there, I learned that dental, pharmaceutical, and medical device companies **loved** to hire sales reps with Enterprise Rent-A-Car on their resume. I thought, *This is my chance! This is how I get rich. This is how I make a lucrative career and how I make my parents proud.*

I quickly finished college in three years, which required a lot of summer classes leaving not a lot of social time. I immediately started applying to any company I could find.

I found a dental sales opportunity in Las Vegas, made it to the final interview, and got a call from the regional manager an hour later and then… I didn't get it.

I told the manager, "Look, I'm fresh out of college. I am capable of succeeding in this role. If you have any openings anywhere in the country, I'll take it."

He paused, and then he said, "If you're willing to move to California, I have a position for you there."

I said, "Done!" and the rest is history.

Fast forward two years later…

I needed to be closer to my family for personal reasons, and I landed a job as a medical device rep in Las Vegas. Little did I know, this job was going to push me into my entrepreneurial journey…

*   *   *

I was at the top of my game. I finished college in three years, and I got a $70,000-a-year job right out of college. Two years later, I almost doubled my pay and was living close to home. Then it hit me. My life from high school until then was running 100 miles per hour, chasing the dollar. I was losing my time and my health for the dollar, which was then the driving factor in what I thought would make me happy.

How silly.

The biggest realization came to me as I was driving home from work, exhausted from working for 50 to 60 hours a week for months. I reflected on if I could see myself doing this until I retired. How do I know that I wasn't thinking about my life in my 20s all wrong? What evidence did I have that I was doing the right thing, in the right way, at the right time? My bank account would say yes. My eating, health, happiness, and relationships would say otherwise. If I used my 20s to grow and experiment with what the world has to offer, would I not be better equipped for the next 10, 20, or 30 years of my life? How can I know what truly makes me happy if I don't continue to do things that I am unsure of? If I stay the path of "success" beating myself to the ground, will I truly understand success? At that moment, I knew **I would**

trade a 6-figure job to find out.

Before making the jump, you should ask yourself, *Am I prepared for the consequences? What would people think? Would anyone in their right mind do what I'm about to do?*

The answer is simple. **It doesn't matter!**

I had to focus on what I would do once I jump. *How would I gain the insight that I needed to find the meaning of success? How do I meet the people who not only prosper financially but spiritually, emotionally, and physically?* I didn't have the time or money to travel all over the world. I needed a "golden ticket," so to speak.

This is why I started my podcast, *Masters of Life*. I knew I had to meet amazing people from all types of industries to get a new point of view on the world. I needed to learn and grow from different cultures, challenges, and experiences.

Starting a business podcast to interview the most daring, strong-willed, ambitious people has opened my eyes to the possibilities of life and business. Imagine having lunch with a successful person every week. Imagine what you can learn. Imagine the knowledge and opportunities I gained outside of the interview. To gain nothing from another person but their stories and experience saved me **decades** of learning.

*　　*　　*

Now, about the names. We, as human beings, do not make the conscious choice to remember names. When we meet new people, we focus on what the conversation is going to be and how we are going to respond. We think about ourselves versus taking a genuine interest in them. We **choose** not to be good at names.

Let me give you an example. Have you ever found someone so attractive, and after a conversation with them, you remember everything they said **including** their name? (Don't lie to me.) That's because all you can think about is them. You'll remember what they wore, what they do, even what they smell like!

We often say, "I'm not good at names," to justify to ourselves why we don't remember the people we meet. The truth is you never made the choice from the beginning. If you take anything from a conversation, make it the person's name. You can ask for clarification on anything else, but asking someone, "What's your name again?" is just embarrassing.

When I was in medical sales, after every cold call, my manager would ask me, "What was the front-desk person's name? What was the assistant's name? What was the doctor's name?" He knew how important it was to know everyone's name, even the "little" people. He understood that we can cold call an account three or four times, but we will not gain any traction or build any meaningful connection if we do not know the names of who we were talking to. How can we expect to sell, to connect, to make someone feel important, without first knowing something as simple as their name?

Dale Carnegie says it best,

> "Remember that a person's name is to that person the sweetest and most important sound in any language."

Dale Carnegie is famous for writing the book *How to Win Friends and Influence People*, which I highly recommend you read if you haven't already. It is a staple in the business and entrepreneur world.

Why do I bring this up? Why is this so important to me? This is the first major lesson I learned in my career, and it is the foundation of any worthwhile relationship.

*   *   *

I have interviewed *Shark Tank* entrepreneurs, cybersecurity/finance CEOs, life coaches, social activists, *Inc. Magazine* entrepreneurs, distinguished Ted speakers, toastmasters, politicians, million-dollar podcasters, luxury real estate moguls, international best-selling authors, social media icons, Las Vegas performers, and Silicon Valley superstars.

I want to share with you the 10 mindset lessons that I found to be the most impactful from my interviews. I tried to avoid the cliché, I tried to avoid the cheesy, and I tried to avoid anything that you could see on a motivational social media post.

No appetizer, no salad, all entrée.

1.   Differentiate Between Real and Imagined Threats

The most successful understand what they need to worry about and what they'll do when it happens. They create a fine line between what they can control and what they can't.

The whole purpose is to live in the **present**. Focus on what actions you can take. We have limited capacity in what we can worry about, so it's best to direct that energy away from the **perceived** future.

Business will throw many variables your way but be mindful and purposeful about what you give your attention to.

"Worry never robs tomorrow of its sorrow, it only saps today of its joy."
~ Leo F. Buscaglia, Author and Motivation Speaker

2. Command Your Circle

This lesson is about creating opportunities for yourself. Too many of us entrepreneurs will go out and try to find mentors or professionals that we want to learn from. This is amazing, but don't forget, **you** are amazing too!

Too many of us want to be "at the table," but the best way to sit with who you want is to invite others! It is possible to have access to whoever you want, but you have to **believe** that your table is worth sitting at.

This is also the basic concept for masterminds, which I strongly suggest everyone joins. A mastermind is a group of people that meet regularly to talk about ideas, problems, and solutions. It is a coalition of minds which is much more powerful than any one individual.

"You're the average of the five people you spend the most time with."
~ Jim Rohn, Motivational Speaker

3. Conflict is Essential

There's a level of humility in listening and learning, especially from people you compete with or disagree with.

Disagree – Being open-minded is one of the hardest things to do because humans have too much **pride**. We love to prove our point and make sure people know our point of view. But the question you constantly have to ask is, *How do I know that I am right?* This isn't self-doubt, but rather a quest for validation. Open your mind to weigh the facts and then make a decision.

Compete – Simon Sinek, in his new book, *The Infinite Game*, talks about "worthy rivals." Instead of focusing on your competition as someone to beat, think about them as who you can learn from, who you can grow from, and who you can ultimately outlast. Learn their strategies and make them your own. Pivot and adapt.

> *"Any fool can know. The point is to understand."*
> ~ Albert Einstein, Physicist

4. Business is a Potluck

This lesson is about understanding that everyone must carry their own weight. As business owners, we continually feel responsible for our employees. We constantly care more about the business than those around us. (Which makes sense, right?) But creating a team that believes in you and wants to see you succeed is the key to a strong foundation.

Don't feel that you have to bring the "food" every time. You are doing a disservice to the growth of your team if you constantly "feed" them. Teach your team to be resourceful. Teach your team to hunt. Teach your team to survive.

> *"Train people well enough so they can leave, treat them well enough so they don't want to."*
> ~ Richard Branson, Virgin Founder

5. Resourcefulness is the Main Ingredient

Hard work never goes out of style. If you think someone is more talented, has an advantage over you, has more money than you, what is your reaction?

The only correct answer is… you are **motivated**.

Resourcefulness is the strongest skill anyone can have,

especially entrepreneurs. I've never met anyone who was resourceful and also envious of others.

Envy is a form of acceptance, and many "wantrepreneurs" have this thought of "if only." That mindset is the death of progress. I am guilty of this. I thought that to start a podcast, I would need to know people and have great connections. (It made me start my podcast two months after the idea.) But we all start somewhere and build. It's easy to forget the build. It's easy to quit.

Remember, those that succeed are the ones that outlast their competition. Business is a cycle, and it is an "infinite game," as Simon Sinek puts it.

Just keep working and believing.

"Work like there is someone working 24 hours a day to take it away from you."
~ Mark Cuban, Entrepreneur

6. Patience is a Form of Action

Learn to love the journey and hard work. Learn to love the process of failure and fighting through the challenges. Being patient is an understanding that it will all pay off.

Work on your craft every day, slowly getting better than the day before. Remember, owners were once founders, teachers were once students, and pros were once amateurs.

"The day you plant the seed is not the day you eat the fruit."
~ Fabienne Fredrickson, Founder of BoldHeart

7. Be Prepared to Accept Opportunity

What is the purpose of opportunity if you don't **grab** it! As entrepreneurs, there is so much freedom that it is important that you look into all the possibilities that will help you grow your business. Not in a million years did I think I would be writing in a book, but I quickly learned the credibility someone can gain by having a book.

The biggest key to this lesson is time management and organization. You have to set up your buckets to receive the rain. Otherwise, you won't have any time to do anything with it. When you are organized and precise with your business, and you run it versus it running you, you open yourself up to capitalizing on opportunities.

"You get to decide where your time goes. You can either spend it moving forward, or you can spend it putting out fires. You decide. And if you don't decide, others will decide for you."
~ Tony Morgan, Author

8. Believe in Something Bigger than Yourself

It might sound tacky at first but knowing your "why" and your purpose is the mindset I found to be the most common among my guests. You have to believe in something. There is no fulfillment in constantly achieving personal goals. As beginning entrepreneurs, freedom and hard work are enough to give us purpose.

However, as you reach certain milestones in your business, money is not a sustainable motivator. You must believe that what you're doing is bigger than who you are. It could be your employees, it could be your family, and it could even be social change. What will get you out of bed is knowing that someone is depending on you. Impacting others will be the key to finding satisfaction in what you do.

"Happiness is really just about four things: perceived control, perceived progress, connectedness (number and depth of your relationships), and vision/meaning (being part of something bigger than yourself)."
~ Tony Hsieh, Founder of *Zappos.com*

9. Don't Settle for a Life Less than what You Are Capable of Living

Make your goals supernatural. Make it exciting. Make it scary. Make it **big, hairy, and audacious!** ...as Jim Collins puts it.

If you know in your gut that you don't see yourself doing what you're doing now, take that leap. Take that chance. Strive for more. Realizing that so much is possible when you decide that you are capable of it. That's what entrepreneurship is all about!

"Have the courage to follow your heart and intuition. They somehow already know what you truly want to become. Everything else is secondary."
~ Steve Jobs, Apple Co-founder

10. Be Successful as a Human Being

The last lesson is what I strive for every day.

Humility, integrity, kindness, and generosity is something we should all work towards and look for in others. Cutting corners and treating people as if they're below you will not get you the people that you need. It might help you make money fast, but like I said earlier, money won't give you lifelong fulfillment.

Throw away your pride. Throw away the thought of being more successful than your neighbor. Throw away the thought of money will define your success. Focus on the right things, and you will attract the right things.

The theory of the compounded effect holds true to be a better human being. Make the hard choices every day to be kind and patient with those around you. Make the hard choice of choosing the right thing to do, even if it'll take your success a little longer. Make the hard choice to take the road less traveled. Do yourself a favor and clear your mind of the thoughts of envy, greed, and pride.

Make friends and connections that last a lifetime because "success" is defined by how you impact those around you. It is defined by how those closest to you will remember you after you're gone from this world.

"Good ethics is good business."
~ Anonymous

This is your time to make a change. This is your time to change the way you think. This is your time to make the conscious decision to be better. It doesn't happen overnight, but progress is progress. Every day you get better, every day you **decide** to be a better human being. Work towards leaving a job that makes you unhappy. Spend more time thinking about what will give you fulfillment, then **execute**.

I will continue to learn and grow from my amazing guests, and I have a long journey ahead of me. I don't know exactly what it will bring, but it **sure** is exciting to think about.

Finally, to whoever is reading this, I wish you the strength, the wisdom, and the discipline to achieve all your goals, but most importantly, I wish you the joy that the process brings.

"Most people overestimate what they can do in one year and underestimate what they can do in ten."
~ Bill Gates, Microsoft Founder

Best of luck,

Christian Rey Perez

About the Author

Christian Perez is the founder of publicity-based, networking platform, MasterCrowd and host of the Masters of Life Podcast. He was a medical device rep before he quit to pursue entrepreneurship.

He lives in Las Vegas, Nevada, with his girlfriend of nine years and mini Goldendoodle, and would love to connect if you are ever in "Sin City." He loves to play chess and basketball in his free time.

He is passionate about organizations like Operation Underground Railroad (focuses on stopping child trafficking) and the National Lymphedema Network (focuses on the treatment and awareness of lymphedema).

Contacts

Email: Christianp@mastercrowd.io
Christianp@mastersoflifepodcast.com

Website: Mastercrowd.io
  Mastersoflifepodcast.com

Instagram: @Christianrey_perez
@MasterCrowd

Facebook: https://www.facebook.com/christian.perez.3766952

LinkedIn: https://www.linkedin.com/in/christian-rey-perez-570aa9a5/

Linktree: linktr.ee/mastersoflifepodcast

Don't Let Fear Rule Your Life

Deb Rosman
Author, Speaker, and Uplifter, USA

"The only thing we have to fear is fear itself."
~ Franklin Delano Roosevelt

December of 1987, I watched as a tall figure headed back by the bedrooms. It was very late, around 2:30 a.m. because of the freezing weather hovering at 13 below zero, I had on sweats, but no socks. I soon found out the man was there to rob us. He quickly took two steps and straddled on top of me. OUCH! He hit me in the back of my head with a firm object. Long fingers encircled my throat as he hissed, "Tell the little girl to go to bed." He then released his grip and stuck me at the base of my skull with a dull knife. To my relief and surprise, my roommate's daughter did as I told her to and went to bed. My relief was short-lived.

The man now reached out and grabbed my behind and I fought to keep panic from rising as I vaguely remembered reading that you should try to not to react in a potential sexual attack. The next few seconds felt like hours. Finally, he shifted his attention back to robbing me. He felt my fingers for rings, asking me where the gold was. I said, "Let me up, and I will get it for you." He hesitated but soon allowed me off the bed, so I was in a standing position, which made me feel better. Next, he demanded my purse and money, which netted him about $1.75 cash. After that, he asked me where my car keys were. I told him I did not know because I had lent my car to a friend earlier. Ironically, he told me they were on the kitchen counter. We proceeded to the kitchen, and I was hopeful that soon he would be gone.

What happened next was truly terrifying.

He told me to show him where I believed my car was parked. As I mentioned earlier, the temperature outside was hovering around 13 below zero, and I was barefoot. The entrance to the building had a metal ramp for handicap accessibility. I pictured the bottoms of my feet being flash-frozen onto that ramp. My fight-or-flight instinct had kicked in, and I was on full alert.

It's amazing how quickly our brains can process a situation and come up with the best possible solution. We began the descent from the second floor. I was positioned a step or two ahead of him. That's when I went for it, and I broke free! Bolting to the door at the bottom of the stairs where our manager lived, I frantically pounded on their door, screaming for my life. In all, the intruder did not find my car, but in addition to the $1.75 cash it cost me $125 to replace the ignition and the door locks.

Experiencing PTSD

I began to experience the classic symptoms of post-traumatic stress disorder (PTSD). I had trouble sleeping and experienced paranoia. I started to carry a knife and my father lent me his handgun. My roommate tried to understand but begged me to give the handgun back to my father. I eventually did, but not before I came close to shooting an innocent person! I had no idea what was happening to me, since PTSD wasn't commonly known. I never sought counseling.

My Epiphany

After months of living in absolute terror, and suffering from paranoia and insomnia, one day, I just realized that I was no longer willing to live like that. Fear can stop us in our tracks and prevent us from living a full and happy life. We often don't pursue our dreams because we become too bogged down with the fear of failure, or we fear being judged by others.

I've always considered myself a fortunate and overall happy person. I would even go so far as to say I'm a bit of a Pollyanna. I wear rose-colored glasses and am usually happy to the point of what others call delusional. I love the fact that we can tint our world by looking through a lens of happiness. I never realized how much control we do have and what a tremendous gift the rose-color glasses are.

The Pollyanna Effect

It's only been in recent years that I stumbled across, what I thought was purely by accident, the LOA principles. If you're not familiar with the term, LOA stands for "Law of Attraction." We've all heard it in any number of ways, such as oft-repeated sayings like "If you can see it, you can be it," or "What you think about, you bring about" these are two of the more common examples. LOA resonates within me because it explains a lot of things, but more importantly, I find it to be incredibly empowering.

A key principle of the Law of Attraction states that we are "responsible" for everything that happens to us because we attract everything into our experience. Does that mean that I somehow attracted my intruder? Yes, in a way, I did, but let's back up for a second. No one in their right mind would intentionally think something bad into their existence, would they?

What Is the Law of Attraction?

In a nutshell, the Law of Attraction says that whatever we focus our attention on most consistently can and will manifest.

In retrospect, I can identify times in my life where I was so negatively focused on "reality" it resulted in manifestations such as a poor love life, bad jobs, and a feeling of being stuck. Law of Attraction has taught me to use my emotions as an indicator. Hence, the importance of being a bit of a Pollyanna. I used to believe that it was important to vent my negative feelings. Now I understand that was just fast-tracking more negative things into my existence. I won't delve too deeply into the principles of the Law of Attraction as there's a wealth of information on it out there. Instead, I will share with you how my personal techniques of LOA have changed my life.

Success Action #1 is to Learn to Love Self

This is learning to love myself just as I am and not for what I think other people want or need me to be for their sake. I've been lucky, born into a loving, blue-collar family – a GM factory-working dad and an amazing, stay-at-home, "crafty" mom. I genuinely enjoyed a happy upbringing. So much so that I'm currently working on my next book entitled, *A Mural in Purple Crayon: Memoirs of a Happy Childhood.*

My parents, along with teachers and mentors over the years, have shaped my beliefs. One of the big beliefs, for me, was coming from a blue-collar background, of which I'm proud, meant that I wasn't ever going to an Ivy League college or getting fast-tracked into a seven-figure job. I now realize that I had placed limitations upon myself.

Success Action #2 is to Stop Comparing Yourself Against Others

One of the most dangerous things we can do is compare ourselves to others. When I was growing up, fashion magazines, television, and movie icons molded a person's image of themselves, much like they do today.

Twiggy, a supermodel, set the tone for what beauty meant. She, like her name, was very tiny – no hips and very thin. Guess who had hips? I hated my shape because I didn't look like her or the other models. Today I can appreciate my curves.

Success Action #3 Is to Live Authentically

Decades were flying by me. I was basically a happy person, or was I just telling myself that? Who did I think I was, to expect more from life than I was experiencing? After years of working hard for other people, although enjoying my life, I grappled with the question, *Is that all there is?* I found myself restless and often feeling empty. Worse I often felt trapped and that is a slippery slope into feeling hopeless.

In 2003, I lost my father, then we learned of my sister's breast cancer. We lost a close family member in 2006 after that my sister passed. The worst was when my mom died in 2008, add to that, my condo burned down in 2010, it was a very stressful time. Was I drawing these negative events into my life? Spoiler alert: I now accept that on many levels I did. I was so focused on all things negative that I kept spiraling out of control.

Don't misunderstand, of course, I had no control over who made their transition, nor did I have anything to do with the condo fire. I was living in such a bad headspace that had anyone suggested LOA to me then, I would only have argued my limitations, and nearing 50 years old I was haunted by the question, *Is this all there is to life and living?*

Success Action #4 is it's Never Too Late to change

Revelation – There's no such thing as too late to go after your dreams! I've always enjoyed writing and sharing what I've written with friends and family. I was in the process of coming to terms with the fact that we are human and that our physical beings have a shelf life.

One of the worst things for me is feeling trapped, whether that's in a relationship or job. If I'm not growing and moving forward, then I'm not living fully an <u>authentic</u> life, whatever it be. I began to make very subtle changes when driving to work. Frequently I was stuck in traffic and downright miserable about it. One day, I began listening to CDs, both music and books that inspired me. I turned my daily commute into a rejuvenating time. It became my happy place; my car was my temple.

During my commute, one day, I was running early for a change. I was relaxed, enjoying my cup of coffee, when I had an impulse to pull off the road. I was very close to the Long Island Sound, a beautiful place. I decided to pull over and enjoy the sunrise while I drank my coffee. It was a magical experience. I look back at that day fondly. What I have learned through my study of the Law of Attraction is that because I was in alignment with my inner being or higher self that is where the impulse came from, glad I followed it. After that I just continued doing things that brought me joy. I experienced a glorious chain of events. The more I paid attention to how I was feeling and actively pursuing happiness, the happier I was.

Success Action #5 Is to Rewrite Your Story

Start thinking new thoughts; rewrite your story. I began to think about my new story – becoming a writer. "If you can see it, you can be it," and "What we think about, we bring about." Do a vision board but keep it to yourself until you reach the point of not caring about what other people think. It is key that you change your perspective if you want change to occur. For example, things always work out for me.

Success Action #6 Is Tiny Changes Add Up

It is so important to live in the moment. How many times have we heard that little chestnut? Sounds great on paper, but how do we accomplish this seemingly monumental task? People who want to be happy often allow themselves to get bogged down with negativity, also known as "reality." I've learned that it only takes a minor shift in attention to feel good, or at least feel better. Many people fall into situations or traps caused by the old rationale that "everyone else is doing this" some examples: *If everyone is complaining about the government, why wouldn't I? Everyone else is whining about not having enough money, so why wouldn't I?* Misery does love company! It reminds me of the classic mother's question, "Well, if all of your friends jump off a bridge, would you?" I think I heard it termed recently as "herd mentality."

Success Action #7 Is to constantly Shift Your Perspective

I finally understood and had perfect clarity about what an authentic life meant to me. The individual soul is multifaceted, and at the end of the day, I needed to focus on my own sparkling self. I am one of many who now realize that self-love and self-care aren't only good things to have, they are critical. In fact, I follow what I term "airline wisdom."

Almost everyone reading this has been on a plane. At some point, they instruct you that, should there be a sudden loss in cabin pressure, an oxygen mask will drop down, but before you can assist anyone else, you must secure your own oxygen mask first.

Power Summary:

- **Love Self** – If you don't feel worthy, then how can you ever expect good things?

- **Stop Comparing Yourself to Others** – Especially in our social-media age. Focus on what is inside of you, not on how you compare to anybody else. You are unique, and that's a gift

- **Live Authentically** – Follow your dreams.

- **Never Too Late** – Change is the only constant in life, and you can always change your life for the better.

- **Rewrite Your Story** – If the image of you doesn't make you happy, you can change the narrative to one that better serves you.

- **Tiny Changes Add Up** – We live moment by moment, so the smallest shift of your focus makes a big difference.

- **Shift Perspective** – People love to challenge you with "reality." What you focus upon is your reality. Put on those rose-colored glasses and enjoy life.

Just like the airplane wisdom dictates, if you want to help anyone else, you must secure your own happiness first. I'm not suggesting that we stop doing everything in our power to do the best job we can or do whatever we can for our loved ones, just filter everything through a rose-colored lense of self-care and happiness first for maximum effectiveness.

Once I put my happiness first and focused on subtle, incremental shifts, I began to feel good most of the time. I did this in a myriad of ways. Most of them were so simple. If I felt like people treated me poorly at the office or on the streets, I would listen to music, which is a fast way to reset your mood. I try to focus moment by moment on making subtle changes until my joy becomes more solid.

What you put out there comes back to you. Whether it's negativity or positivity, it is what you get in return and a little bit of practice goes a long way. Before you know it, by using my action steps, you will find yourself much happier. The key principle of LOA is not letting fear rule your life. While fear can be an essential survival instinct, we don't do things we want to do because we fear what other people think or fear repercussions. When you're focused on just being happy and content, all those fears fall away.

Today, my emotions are my guide. Being human, I make mistakes, but I quickly forgive myself now and move on. I embrace the little things because life is a continuous stream of moment-by-moment experiences. I live more fully in the present because I know I have so much more control over my emotions, and so can you, starting right now.

Let me leave you with one of my favorite quotes that has inspired me to live fearlessly because life really is what you think about and focus on.

"The only thing we have to fear is fear itself."
~ Franklin Delano Roosevelt

Deb Rosman

About the Author

I spent years in the corporate sector working for the likes of JP Morgan Investment Bank and various international energy trading shops. I realized that while I enjoyed the high-octane life, I was not living an authentic one. I am a writer, a seeker of joy and a change agent. My debut book, *The Grieving Heart: A Collection of Poetry and Prose about Loss, Hope, and Living* in 2019, was written to encourage the grieving process as I believe once you have embraced and worked through this process, you become free to live life fully again.

Contacts

Business Name: Deb Rosman – Author, Speaker, and Up-Lifter

Website: debrosman.com

Email: debrosman1@gmail.com

***Facebook*:** www.facebook.com/public/Deb-Rosman

***Instagram*:** www.instagram.com/debrosmanauthor

***LinkedIn*:** www.linkedin.com/in/deb-rosman-88538783

***Twitter*:** twitter.com/DebraRosman

Thrive Global: thriveglobal.com/authors/deb-rosman

Services: Public Speaker, Wellbeing Coach, Corporate Speaker – The Power of Kindness

Ideal Clients: Seekers of life and corporations who wish to improve the quality of their work environment.

Let Go and Set Yourself Free

Captain Hany Hanana
First Malaysian Certified KonMari Consultant
and Mindful Coach, Malaysia

"The space in which we live should be for the person we are becoming now, not for the person we were in the past."
~Marie Kondo

The Meltdown

They said I was lucky. I had the luxury of living every human's dream. I made it through to become an airline pilot when I was barely 21. Everyone knows it is a high-paying job, and your life will be successful and smooth sailing. That's what they said. So, I did follow through with it. I was earning when my friends were still struggling with their college assignments. Like any other high-earners, I spent and lived the life I aspired to live.

So, you need to know I came from a middle-class, working family where every cent was carefully calculated, thanks to my frugal dad. I was even made to pay for my own driving license when my friends' licenses were being sponsored as a graduation gift from their parents. Almost every other little expense was being written into an "I OWE YOU" list. But the good thing is, I lived spending only on necessities. I thought I was very well taught to spend wisely. Well, at least that was how I was spending the first six months of my salary.

Then, I saw my friends spending their money on luxury cars and luxury holidays, gadgets, hobbies, adventures, and their so-called "pilot thing." I started to doubt myself for being satisfied. I thought, *Why don't I get myself one? I am more than capable of spending.* Watching their extravagance made me forget that I came from a middle-class, working family, that my dad had retired, and I was now the breadwinner. Every penny counts. My calculations did not consider that those friends around me came from a wealthy family, who could spend because everything would be "paid for" in case they were broke at the end of the month.

Of course, I needed to cope with the commitments I had put myself in.

Everyone, including myself, thought we were very well paid. We got to live an extraordinary life. No one needed to know I was living on credit cards, and I was the definition of "stone broke." I continued living the "aspiring life," paying credit cards at the end of the month and then topping them up with personal loans and whatever the bank offered.

We lived on our flying allowance, which adds up to a fat amount compared to our basic pay. But, yes, I needed to go to work. I couldn't afford to be sick or risk any disciplinary mistakes. No. Never. The money issue did not bother me at all, except for one nagging thought, *Why didn't I have money when I was getting paid more than double, on average, relative to my non-pilot friends?*

The Turning Point

One wonderful day, I went for a flight. It was a beautiful flight. I had great company that night. We ate, talked, laughed, and that night wasn't a "long" night as we would always describe it. Eight hours passed by with the help of such fantastic weather, clear skies, and a starry night, and everything was cooperating well until just before landing. Then, I was caught in an incident.

Passengers might have been oblivious to the mistake, but it was an error that could cost me my career. There's always a saying, "Laugh too much, and you will cry later." It had caused me to be grounded for two long months. I was lucky. It was my first mistake, so I was given a final warning letter and had to undergo probation for one year. I didn't lose my job. I knew God was giving me a second chance.

Two long months without allowance. Nothing left for me to spare, except to again spend using the credit cards. Deep shit, I know. But how was I going to survive if this continued even for another month? Okay, now let's find out.

So, I started searching online for "How to Live a Simple Life," "How to Organize Your Life," etc., etc. I then stumbled upon "Declutter Your Life the KonMari Way." Everything after that was KonMari and Marie Kondo. Who is she? Why is she so famous? Why is she everywhere? Or is it just the analytics thing?

The Impact

I got caught into obsessing over her in just a few days after that. After a thorough reading and taking lots and lots of notes from her book (literally!), I started my KonMari Festival, following each and every step. It was a dreaded, long, and draining but surprisingly a very motivating process. It was magical! I was trying to declutter my home, but I ended up decluttering my mind and soul as well. It was a life-changing magic.

Remember I had nothing to spare just days before I read her book? Then, out of nowhere, I had extra cash to spend! That's surprising, right? It was truly magic! It felt like the money had fallen from the sky!

Her method had a significant impact on me — to my life as a whole and to everything I see. It was a completely new world. I realized, actually, I hardly appreciated anything I had. I was in a constant search for better things in my life to feel satisfied. Well, actually, I was trying to find the missing pieces to complete the puzzle.

I began keeping only things that spark joy, the things that I really appreciate, or something that had meaning and purpose in my life. I let go of more than 30 large bags full of things that I found unjoyful in the process. I had things that I've kept for over 20 years, just because. I didn't know why. Some had never even been used.

I began to use each of the things that I kept, started appreciating each item, giving it the meaning and purpose, and understanding why it was bought initially. It was a fascinating journey. I began to declutter my social platform, my feeds, and the people around me. It felt amazing.

Just six months down the road from being broke, penniless, full of debt, I started to be able to save up quite a massive amount of money, which I had never imagined before. I never thought it was possible. That was my greatest achievement in life at that particular time. I was looking back to life before that unfortunate flight. It would never have changed me if it did not happen that day.

To prove my success, I managed to settle close to a quarter of my debt balance. I managed to organize my life, started to plan my life, and got everything in order – finally! So, for the first time, I got to see the whole picture. I planned to settle everything in less than five years. That was the plan. I've always thought that I needed to continue living my previous life and work and sweat it out until I was 65. That was still in my mind until I found this magic.

The Freedom

Since I first started my tidying journey, I've always wanted to help people find their purpose in life. It had changed my perspective in life. I had always been a self-centered person, and this journey had taught me to become a person who loved to give back. I want to be a person with a purpose in this world, to leave my footprint, to be able to change someone's life even in the smallest way possible. I dream to inspire and aspire others. I finally found that purpose in life.

I was always shy to tell anyone I was a pilot. I wasn't really proud, perhaps because there's a lot of weight that came together with it. But I was really enjoying the extra miles I did with what I had earned. I am proud to be able to give back.

The year 2020 had been a challenging year. It had taught me that what I had was enough. I keep reflecting on how I can support others and how I can ease their life. I was happy and content until I received my retrenchment notice. It was so sudden and unexpected. I was no longer needed in the company for the next ten days! There goes my five-year-to-debt-free plan.

So what now? Amazingly, I was as calm as ever. I didn't realize I was setting my heart to be content all these years. I was set free, and it feels like a burden had lifted from me. It was an incredible feeling. I thought I was supposed to be sad or miserable or depressed, but none of it actually happened.

I am a free bird, and I can do whatever I want from now on. So, I chose to continue helping others because that's what makes me happy! I want others to achieve the freedom I had achieved. But first, declutter your mind, set your vision in life, and you are good to go.

From now on, it is always about finding joy in our lives. I want to share the beauty of decluttering and setting your goal. It is all about appreciating the current life we live in, not about keeping everything from the past and thinking that we might need it in the future. It is choosing what matters most at the present time – choosing joy over everything else. It is about a calm mind and self-reflection on our belongings. It is about gratitude.

Being calm.
Being content.
Being relieved.
Being confident.
Being meaningful.

I am now continuing my KonMari journey, but this time, on a bigger mission. I can practice and get recognition for my work done. I want to share the beauty of decluttering, like how the method had impacted my life.

When I first started, my family and friends were skeptical about me doing a "cleaning" job. I was furious. Nobody takes me seriously. But I know I have a bigger mission, and I am always a high achiever. So, I took another path. Since I didn't get enough support from people close to my heart, I should open up my heart to others, right? So that was what I did.

I started reaching out to people to share the beauty of this method and how to live to appreciate everything we have in our life. Surprisingly, I received tons of inquiries seeking assistance in kicking off their decluttering journey or people who simply needed help getting on track and organizing their lives. It is truly a global issue.

There are so many out there who thought they were on-track and everything was alright, but actually, they have something at the back of their mind that is blocking their potential. The method is about self-reflection. I have talked to a number of people who tried to declutter, but they still feel lost. People who reached out knew that they are making an investment by hiring me, and I am glad I am able to make a change and make a difference in someone's life – the thing I have been looking for all these years.

The Ordinary World

Walking down my path wasn't easy. Growing up, I was always seen as a strong and independent person; hence I have developed myself to be one. I was always living to people's expectations of me. When I started my career in a male-dominant job, I was expected to do what they expect me to do. Some even told me that they learn about flying more at the bar and their social trips rather than in the cockpit itself. I just refuse to do what they do due to the sole reason our interests do not align.

I did a lot of sewing during my free time, and I was looked down on for that. They thought sewing is a low-class hobby compared to their high-class luxury bikes and cars, and even their mountain climbing and luxury holidays. Some even blamed my sewing activities as the cause of my incident. How is that possible, right? They didn't know that sewing makes me calm and content. I am able to give and make the receiver happy. That was when I thought, well, perhaps, *This is not my place*.

Although I needed the numbers in my bank account, I thought there should be other ways to reach that goal. I was searching for my freedom and purpose. I didn't have the guts to let go of what I had. Again, people would question. Nobody knows what took place in my heart and mind. I was supposed to help myself.

Then, I realized everyone needs support or a mentor in their life to guide them. I want to be one where people can come and reach out. Being a mindful coach makes me realize that I could offer the support they needed. That is what we need in life. Sometimes, we don't have enough support from the people around us, hence the need to reach out. We need to find a person who can help us shine through. You need to reach out. Get yourself organized and declutter for a better life. That was just what I did. I was able to shift my mindset and focus on what makes me happy, and by being a coach, to make others happy! I made this choice confidently, and I am proud of myself. I am happier and wealthier now, even if I can't call myself a commercial widebody pilot anymore.

Key Lessons and Words of Wisdom

I've learned the hard way. Experience is the best teacher. I couldn't agree more. I realized that writing down our plans and goals will attract our unconscious mind to work towards that goal. It doesn't need to be perfectly done; it just has to be done.

In less than a year, I was able to be an authority, expert, and influencer in my field, which would not have been possible if I did not let go of my past. I dream to continue guiding anyone and, if possible, everyone in reaching their goals and purpose in life.

#1 – Take one step at a time.

Be easy on yourself. Do one thing at a time, and you will reach your goal sooner than what you expected.

#2 – Plan, plan, plan, and imagine!

Every single thing begins with planning. Set a goal. Be specific and detailed. Imagine living your goal, and you are one step away from success! Just one more step to success!

#3 – Let go.

The key to moving forward is to let go of the past. Let go of anything that stops you from reaching your ideal lifestyle.

#4 – Always remind yourself and find motivation.

Ask yourself, *What is your ideal lifestyle? Why do you want to achieve that goal? Why do I need to get there soon?* Give a time frame to achieve it, and you will achieve it!

#5 – Invest in a coach.

Why would I? I can do it myself! A coach is there for a reason. To get you there faster. It was a long and exhaustive road for me. Instead of doing it the hard way, why not take a shortcut and get professional advice, right? Reach your goals faster with proper guidance and someone to support you through your journey. It is an investment for greater returns!

#6 – Set a time frame.

We always expect results when we do something. This is especially important for a huge goal. Would you want it to take a lifetime to complete so you will not see your change until you're 88? Or do you want to do it now? Set a time timeline. Declutter everything within two months and see the difference. Don't take too long, or you will never achieve.

The Reward

I kissed goodbye to flying the sky, but now, I soar! I feel trusted more than ever. People are reaching out to me to get help in decluttering their lives! My consultancy business is getting stronger, and I can complete that five-year-to-debt-free journey even earlier. I get to have my own sewing studio and set up my consultancy office just like how I wanted. I get to spend my time sewing, conducting sewing classes, giving talks, and at the same time helping others declutter and reach their goals and dreams!

I get to organize my own time and do what I love to do, instead of keeping up to people's expectations! How wonderful life is!

> *"People cannot change their habits without first changing their way of thinking. No matter how wonderful things used to be, we cannot live in the past. The joy and excitement we feel here and now are more important."*
> ~ Marie Kondo

Success Action

1. Commit yourself to decluttering.

2. Prepare your mind; be willing to change.

3. *"Change your thoughts, and you change your world"* ~Norman Vincent Peale

4. Imagine your ideal lifestyle; write it down.

5. E.g., I want to set up a beautiful dinner table and have a home-cooked meal every day.

6. Take action. Begin decluttering. Follow the right order.

I wish you all the best in finding your dreams and reaching your goals in life! Remember to declutter first, then keep only what sparks joy!

Take care and best wishes,

Hany Hanana

About the Autor

Captain Hany Hanana is a Certified KonMari Consultant and Mindful Coach who currently lives in Malaysia.

She was formerly a widebody commercial pilot who flew the Airbus 320, 330, and 340 for over 12 years. Her passion for tidying and helping others declutter their mind and life has brought her into becoming a KonMari Consultant.

Other than helping others declutter, she spends her spare time managing her sewing studio and conducting sewing classes for adults and children.

Contacts

Websites: https://tidyhabit.com/

https://captaincrafter.com/

Instagram: https://www.instagram.com/neatandtidyspace/

https://www.instagram.com/captain.crafter

Make the Choice and Chase Your Dreams

Jessica Fox
Master Transformation Coach, USA

*"The future belongs to those who believe in the beauty of
their dreams."*
~ Eleanor Roosevelt

Hitting Rock Bottom

You have two choices: filing for bankruptcy or insolvency."

I sat across a large, beautiful desk as she explained my options. I glanced out the windows of the downtown high-rise, and I was overwhelmed by the gloom of the day and the hopeless situation I was in. The guilt, the shame, the embarrassment, and the sense of failure was overwhelming. I could hardly concentrate on the information being shared. After losing my health, career, and income, I didn't believe I could sink any lower.

I was wrong.

I was thirty-four years old with two children and one on the way. My husband was struggling to keep a roof over our heads. I hadn't worked in over a year due to illness. Now we were facing the reality that we may lose our home and vehicles on top of everything we had lost the previous year. I thought I had already hit rock bottom when I burned-out of my career, and here I was, even lower, facing even more devastating consequences. The weight of my reality was so heavy that I just sat in that office and cried. Clearly, the agent was used to this response and had tissues ready. She graciously waited in reassuring silence while I worked through my emotions.

I left the office in defeat, having signed the papers that would get the creditors off our backs while allowing us to keep our home. I sat down in my car and began to sob, and that grief quickly turned to anger. My anger at the situation, anger at myself, anger at God. The anger exploded out of me in a fury of yelling at my steering wheel:

"Why is this happening to us?"
"Life is supposed to be better than this!"
"What did we do wrong?"
"Why can't anything go right?"
"I can't do this anymore!"
"What's the point of any of this?"

My anger exhausted and feeling hopeless and dejected, I made my way home from my appointment, embarrassed and alone.

I Had Become a Victim

A week or so after the shock of signing insolvency papers had worn off, my husband and I sat down to figure out how we would manage our monthly payments and have the hard conversation about how we had gotten into the situation and circumstances we were facing. Through our discussion, we noted that some of our circumstances were out of our control, some came because we followed misguided advice, and some were the result of poor decision-making on our part. But rather than taking responsibility and looking for solutions, I developed a "Why me?" attitude. I became a victim of my circumstances, blaming everyone and everything for the situation we were facing. I was angry, and at the same time, I felt defeated and wondered if our life would ever change. The truth here is that I had taken on this victim role more than once in my life. While it felt completely disempowering to be a victim, I didn't actually realize that is what I was doing – until now!

Enough was Enough

The weeks following filing insolvency awakened me to the fact that I had been playing the victim to the circumstances of my life. It was like a thick fog suddenly lifted from my heart and brain, and I could see the consequences that playing the victim had not only in my external world but on my internal one.

With the fog of "Why me?" lifted, I could see how I had surrendered my personal power and my responsibility to be the creator of my own life. I could see how far I had strayed from my sense of purpose and how I had lost belief in the beauty of my dreams. I knew at that moment that I had a choice: to continue playing the victim or to take back my dreams, my power, and control as the creator of my life.

Enough was enough, and I chose to take my power back!

The Revelations

I would love to tell you that leaving victimhood, reclaiming my dreams, and stepping into my power was as easy as flipping a light switch, but it wasn't. I had developed habits of thought, belief, and behavior that served my victim mindset. It took time, effort, determination, and the intentional re-programming of my mind with the help of both a coach and counselor to me get back to the woman I knew I was and desired to be again. There were several revelations of truth that I learned as I healed and recommitted to my true self that I want to share with you right now.

Revelation 1: Self-Forgiveness is Necessary

I cannot stress how important forgiving yourself is when you realize that you have allowed yourself to slip into victimhood. Self-forgiveness is the first step that creates internal space for you to take back your personal power. Even more so, if you are reading this and realize that, maybe, you have been playing a victim of your life and circumstances longer than you would like to admit. Getting caught up in the circumstance of life is something we have all experienced to one extent or another, but we have a choice. We can choose to experience more out of life. We can choose to learn from our circumstances and create new opportunities rather than succumb to them. We can choose to forgive ourselves for the ways we have fallen short, letting go of the past, and we can choose to embrace a better future.

Revelation 2: "Everything is figureoutable"

Marie Forleo says:

> *"No matter what you're facing, you have what it takes to figure <u>anything</u> out and become the person you're meant to be. You wouldn't have the dream if you didn't already have what it takes to make it happen."*

You need to read that again! You wouldn't have the dream if you didn't already have what it takes to make it happen. Even though you may feel like you've lost your sense of self or lost the belief that your dreams could come true, you need to know that because you have the dreams you have, they are yours to realize in this life. When you step into your power and go from "I can't!" to "How can I?" the way to realize the dream and vision you have for your life will open to you. Your dreams are not lost, they are absolutely figureoutable!

Revelation 3: What You Think, You Create

Whatever you choose to believe about yourself and your circumstance is true. If you believe it is a learning opportunity that can change your life for the better, it is. If you believe it is just evidence that nothing ever goes right and nothing will change, it is. For good or bad, what you think and what you put your mental energy towards will come to pass in your life. We always have a choice: Will I be a victim of my circumstance and perpetuate a victimized existence, or will I put the power of my thoughts to work and create a better future for me to experience? When we understand the reality of this statement, "What I think, I create," it puts into motion the desire for constructive, life-giving thinking that transforms our lives in remarkable ways.

Revelation 4: Anchors Are a Must

One of the strategies I teach all my clients is to anchor their commitment to their vision, dreams, and goals with something in the physical environment that is triggered by the five senses. It could be a song, a smell, a picture, or a phrase. The anchor should be meaningful, powerful, and somewhere accessible. The purpose of this anchor is to help keep you focused and to help you when you slip back into those old habits of thought and belief. By using anchors throughout the process of reclaiming your dreams and your personal power, you are setting yourself up for success by reminding yourself of who you truly are and the life you desire to have.

Revelation 5: Recommit to Your Dream and Vision

The choice to no longer be a victim to your circumstances and step back into your personal power needs to be followed by a recommitment to a dream and vision you have for your life. For some, it's about creating a dream and vision that you've never allowed yourself to have before. For others, it's reconnecting and fanning into flame the embers of a dream that was almost extinguished. What is amazing in this process is that the spark of dreams and visions quickly transforms into a burning desire, and with a burning desire comes energy, intention, direction, and focus.

As I began to implement the lessons I learned from those five revelations and really allow my sense of purpose, passions, and dreams to begin directing my choices, my life very quickly turned around. And here I am today, writing this chapter as proof that when you let go of being a victim and step into your power, dreams really do come true.

Dreams Do Come True

In a way, it is almost surreal how different my life is now from the day I cried and screamed in defeat at my steering wheel. I reconnected with my heart and purpose to empower women, and now I get the privilege of serving hundreds of entrepreneurial moms as a Master Transformational Coach and by launching the Thriving in Business and Motherhood Movement. I have recently moved into the house of my dreams, and in less than a year, I had the honor of fulfilling a lifelong dream of not only becoming a published author but becoming an international bestselling author with two more titles being released on the heels of the first. I also had the privilege of being a featured on a *TED-Ed* stage, and all of this during a pandemic.

I look at how quickly my life changed with a sense of awe and profound gratitude, and I know it is because I made a choice – a choice to embrace my power and purpose, follow my dream and vision, and go for it! The result, you, dear reader, are experiencing with me, in this moment, today.

Inspired Actions

If you are ready to make the choice and make your dreams a reality, I have a few simple, implementable action steps for you to consider.

1. **Create a Plan**. Once you choose to let go of the victim mentality, it is so important to know where you desire to go. Know the big picture. Know what you desire to experience in this life and align yourself, your belief, and your actions with the outcome you desire to experience in this life. Even if you don't know how you will get from where you are to where you want to be, creating the plan and trusting the process will produce fruit in your life that is better than you could have ever imagined.

2. **Surround Yourself with the Right People**. For better and for worse, the people in our life influence our mindset, our decisions, our confidence, and direction. Make sure to surround yourself with those that believe in the dream that you are holding for your future and ones that will call you out of playing a victim when less than ideal circumstances come your way. Your community, friends, and mentors need to hold you to the dreams and potential you have been created to experience. So, don't settle for less when it comes to the people you surround yourself with.

3. **Own your Personal Power**. We only have one life, and we might as well make it our best. Recognize that when you live in a mindset or heart-set that is less than the fullness of your purpose, power, and potential, you won't experience all that this life has to offer. So, don't settle for anything less and walk as who you have been created to be – the only you that will ever walk on and change this amazing world.

You can do this! This is your life! These are your dreams! It is your future!

Make your choice today and live this life to the fullest.

No matter what you're facing, you have what it takes to
figure anything out and become the person you're meant to
be. You wouldn't have the dream if you didn't already have
what it takes to make it happen.
~ Marie Forleo

Jessica Fox

About the Author

My name is **Jessica Fox**, #1 International Bestselling Author of *Yes I Can!*, featured *TED-Ed* Presenter, and Master Transformational Coach.

I am passionate about empowering mothers to fully realize their purpose, power, and potential. My mission is simple: to help mothers embrace their entrepreneurial dreams and create a work-at-home lifestyle that is more than dry shampoo and coffee!

I'm a wife of one and a mama of three. Most days, you will find me in my comfiest jeans, attempting to accomplish something work-related amid the chaotic hum of life with a young family and dogs. I am a lover of musicals, *Harry Potter*, good coffee, and Jesus. It isn't uncommon to find me lost in the woods or lost in my never-satisfied book addiction.

I help entrepreneurial moms who struggle with time management, productivity, and self-confidence.

When they work with me, they learn to master their time, experience more focused, productive working hours, and tap into their purpose, power, and potential.

My coaching helps the entrepreneurial mama to be in love with her business, in love with her family and ultimately, in love with herself.

If you are ready to love your business, love your family, and love yourself, please check out my links on the next page.

Contacts

If having a breakthrough in your business and motherhood is something that interests you, please check out my links below.

Grab your copy of *Yes I Can!* here: https://bit.ly/36c44W5

Check out my *TED-Ed* feature here: https://bit.ly/3lb2FFr

Book your Free Time to Thrive Breakthrough Session:
https://bit.ly/timewithjessfox

Receive your Free Gift, The Thriving in Business & Motherhood Handbook:
http://bit.ly/thrivinghandbook

Join my *Facebook* Group: https://bit.ly/thrivingWAHMs

LinkedIn: www.linkedin.com/in/jessicafoxcoaching

Instagram: https://www.instagram.com/jessicaruthfox

Email: jessicafoxcoaching@gmail.com

What Fuels Your Fire?

Matt Brauning
Entrepreneur, USA

"The opposite of procrastination isn't motivation… it's always vision."
~ Matt Brauning

I'm six years old, and I'm standing behind this huge oak tree on my first day of kindergarten. As I watched these kids playing in the playground, right then and there and I knew I had a fatal flaw. I knew I couldn't walk up and just play with those kids the same as they would play with each other. It wasn't possible. I was different. I didn't know why at the time, and in fact, it took me years to discover.

That first year of school, all the kids seemed to make friends so easily. Not me. I couldn't bear the pressure of walking up to someone, saying hi, and getting rejected. It wasn't just because I was shorter than most, or wore hand-me-down clothes from my cousin, to my brother, to me. It was because deep inside, I felt different, like I was on the outside looking in.

Plus, I asked too many questions. When kids would play with each other, they would play on the swings, and I would be wondering, *How do they get the swings there?* and, *Why do they pick that side of the playground?* When they played in the sandbox, I wondered, *How they got all the sand in one spot? Did they use a truck? How did that work?* I asked so many questions, and I was different.

When Elon Musk, the founder of SpaceX and co-founder of Tesla and *PayPal* was interviewed recently, he said, "When I was a kid, I was scared that they were gonna come and take me away. I was scared because I was different, and I knew I thought differently than everyone else. If they found out how different I was, they would know I don't belong here."

This was the first day I knew that I didn't belong. But it wasn't the last.

Every year in school it seemed to get worse and worse. Sometimes I would get bullied a bit, nothing too serious, just making fun of my name, or my height, or something like that. I could actually take that pretty well.

What was worse? When they would forget to pick on me at all. Becoming invisible was the worst of all. I had a couple friends here or there, but moving to junior high, then on to high school, friends got fewer and further between. I had one friend to talk to, but still, that nagging feeling was ever-present – you don't belong.

I graduate, and start working immediately for these two brothers in the mortgage business. Joe and Ed taught me everything. They really became my mentors. I didn't know what a mentor was then, but thank God for them! I learned all the ins and outs of the business, and within a couple years, started making a pretty serious income too.

Friends came a bit in and out of my life, girlfriends here and there too, but mostly only if a girl took an interest in me (although I literally have no idea how that happened!)

The day after my 22nd birthday, all that changed. I wake up in the morning like any other day, get showered and dressed, and head out of my beach house on my way to the mortgage office. Sitting on the bottom steps of my front stairs right outside my house was my boss Ed.

"Matthew, we need to talk…," he said.

He laid in on me. We weren't a good fit anymore after nearly five years. I shouldn't worry about coming in today or tomorrow. Really, I shouldn't worry about coming back at all.

My last check got handed to me, and I received a wish of "luck with my future endeavors."

What do I do now? I have nowhere to go, no one to call.

For five days, I sat at home alone, not knowing what to do with my life.

Then the craziest idea popped into my head. The voice said, *You should start your own mortgage business.*

I could hear my inner voice as clear as if it came from the television, and I knew it was the right thing to do. So, at the tender age of 22, I started my first business from my second bedroom in my beach house in Corona Del Mar, CA.

Within a few weeks, I hire my first employee to help with prospecting and sales. Then my second. After a couple months, I hire a processor to help with operations, and we move into a real office within six months.

Then, a funny thing happened. For the first time, I didn't feel alone or like I was crashing someone else's party. I was the one with the party, and people wanted to be a part of it. Incredible!

Being into personal development, attending Tony Robbins seminars, and studying things like NLP (neuro-linguistic programming), I got very interested in why and how entrepreneurs like myself start the ventures we start.

Over the last 19 years, I've started four different companies, and all of them for different reasons. In fact, I believe every visionary, innovator, and entrepreneur has a deep motivation for creating what they create in the world.

Let me give you an example...

You don't have to be a Ph.D. to know what fuels your car. After all, most of us depend on gasoline for getting around every day. But do you know what fuels a steam engine? Sure, steam is the obvious answer, but it's not exactly true. Steam is what activates the pistons, but it's only present when water is boiling. And to boil water, you need a heat source.

Traditional steam locomotives are equipped with an important feature called a "firebox." Essentially, it's a large, metal container where a fire burns and heats the water in the boiler. When the water starts boiling, it makes pressurized steam, which creates movement. Here's the interesting part – a firebox can be filled with a variety of fuels. In the steam engine's heyday, the Brits were partial to coal, the Americans favored wood, and at various times in history, oil or sugar byproducts have also been used to make those iron giants chug. The fuel used was determined by what was most available, and availability depended on where and when the trains were running.

As a passionate trailblazer, you also have a firebox. It sits at the core of who you are, and it's more than just your personality. It's what drives you and makes you hungry to build something significant. Call it "gusto," call it "heart" – whatever it is, one thing is clear: it's powerful! The problem is that we tend to look over it. We don't take the time to open the firebox and see what's inside. We continue to run and push, but we don't really know what exactly is running and pushing us.

As a leadership consultant and business coach, I've met a lot of unique people. The reason they're unique is because they come from different places, and they grew up at different times. Their environments helped shape their personalities and their motivations. It dictated their fuel in the same way that circumstance dictated the fuel used in steam engines 150 years ago.

In other words, every visionary and entrepreneur has a firebox, but the fuel inside is different. That is, your motivations for starting and initiating are derived from a highly specified set of variables that are unique to you.

This is why I wrote my first new book in over ten years. It is called *The Firebox Principle: The 7 Drives That Fuel Every Entrepreneur.* I started researching the stories of great entrepreneurs from yesterday and today. Crazy enough, I found that every single "origin story" (as I like to call them since I'm a huge superhero fan) fell into one of only seven different patterns. Every startup's story has embedded deep within it one of these seven, and understanding your motivation, or "fuel," can truly transform your business and your culture.

Based on this concept, I've created a Firebox Profile Quiz to help identify your primary drive as a leader. Head over to http://fireboxbook.com and try taking The Firebox Quiz. You will learn about what motivates you in this particular enterprise as well as strengths and weaknesses to watch out for. You will also discover your primary drive's need, its biggest fear, its lifetime goal, and what we call its "reflection": how you want to be seen by others.

Head over right now. It's free and will really help you apply the Firebox Principle for best results. Then come right back, and we will move on forward in this chapter!

*　　*　　*

So, now that you are back and without further ado, here are the seven Firebox drives. See which one (or multiple ones) you relate to most, but first, make sure you have taken the quiz referenced above so you can compare your results.

Significance Drive

This drive finds its roots in the soil of comparison. Individuals and entrepreneurs with a primary Significance Drive fueling them have usually spent time with other successful people. At one point in their lives, they have observed the success of a parent or an important figure around them, which caused them to question their own ability and worth. One important variation in this scenario is whether the urge to define one's self comes directly from another person or indirectly. When a successful person or group of people directly question one's ability to succeed, they find the need to prove their value to the unbelieving party. In cases where the pressure is indirect, an individual asks the same question internally and feels the need to prove something to themselves.

Leaders who share this motivation are Rupert Murdoch, Vince McMahon, and Alexander Graham Bell – and me. For me, it wasn't my family, but my first mentor who I watched succeed. I unconsciously wanted to prove that I, too, was worthy of success.

Artisan Drive

I don't paint. I don't sing. I don't write music, sculpt, dance, or really do any other creative art in my life. But, put me on stage to speak or train, and I'm in heaven. Although I get paid quite well by entrepreneurs all the way to Fortune 100 companies to do this, secretly, I would do it for free. I love it, and I always want to make it better!

I could do any business in the world right now. I could sell tires, I could run a dry cleaner, or I could even own another real estate brokerage. But when I get to dream up new and improved workshops, retreats, and keynote talks, I get into an artist's flow and nearly disappear.

Leaders who share this motivation are Warren Buffet, novelist Jane Austen, and Steve Jobs.

The problem sometimes (especially early on) was charging for what I love to do, and often, it's hard for an artist to see the forest for the trees. I can get wrapped up creating the best story for a keynote talk and perhaps miss the big picture of marketing myself for dates three months from now. Keeping a schedule and a structure can be a challenge for the artisan drive.

World Impact Drive

There used to be a show on TV in the 90s called *Lois and Clark: The New Adventures of Superman.* Dean Cain played Clark Kent (and Superman), and in this version of the Superman story, Clark was the poster boy for good in the world. He was more than just a great guy; he was a "superman," quite literally. He had no flaws, and his motives were always good.

Although I don't think there's anyone on the planet who is as perfect as Clark Kent was in that TV show, there is an aspect of the World Impact Drive that includes real-life heroism and altruistic motives. I'm not talking about people with superpowers or even the brave individuals who serve our country. I'm talking about people who see something wrong in the world and make it their mission to create something that will fix it.

Leaders who share this motivation are Elon Musk, Dr. Martin Luther

King, Jr, and Mary Kay Ash (Mary Kay).

If you want to make the world a better place, and you can't help but live in the future, you might be driven by this fire drive.

Contribution Drive

It's hard to avoid criticism when your initiative or business venture reaches a certain size. It seems as if people will always question the motives of a successful person. While most people could reasonably be criticized for having ulterior or multiple motives, those with a dominant Contribution Drive are able to dodge those arrows. Accusations don't stick to them, and questions about their intentions are easily answered.

This drive is 100 percent pure, and it makes for a clean Firebox. There isn't a trace of doubt that starters and creators with dominant Contribution Drives built their enterprise with others in their best interest. These are people who see others in need and create a project or entity to help them.

Leaders who share this motivation are Blake Mykoskie (TOMS shoes), Bono (U2), and Reshma Saujani (Girls Who Code).

If your main focus, the thing that keeps you up at night, are the problems of the people, you might relate to this fire drive most.

Spiritual Drive

Being religious may have less to do with this drive than you think. The Spiritual Drive is not about adherence to the practices of a religion or an institution. It's more about the presence of an inner calling. You have a dominant Spiritual Drive, which means you have a personal connection with a higher being – whether it be God, Buddha, or the universe – and you follow the voice you sense inside.

At times, these individuals feel a calling to pursue their initiative, and at other times, the calling is to pursue something else through their initiative. Whether it's a means or an end, these individuals believe that what they're doing is inspired by something greater than themselves.

Leaders who share this motivation with you are Mother Teresa, C.S. Lewis, and Chip and Joanna Gaines.

Thrive Drive

This drive comes from a common place for most. First, the Thrive Drive is all about becoming better, and secondly, it's about human nature. Everyone who carries this drive within them has experienced the pain of lack at one point or another. For some people, they grow up in poverty, and for others, they were simply not able to do the things they wanted at one point in their lives. Out of that sense of dissatisfaction, the Thrive Drive is born. You want more!

Leaders who share this motivation with you are Tony Robbins, Jay Z, and Andrew Carnegie.

Avenger Drive

According to legend, it was the power of human emotion in a business setting that has fueled the long-lasting rivalry between the Lamborghini and Ferrari car companies.

Ferruccio Lamborghini was an entrepreneur who was making a living re-purposing old World War II engines into tractors. As he became more successful, he rewarded himself with the purchase of a sports car. Ferraris were highly esteemed, and Ferruccio was fond of their product.

So in 1958, he went to purchase one. As he drove around in his new prize, he noticed (as a mechanic himself) that there were a few improvements that could be made in the assembly of the vehicle he purchased. Since Enzo Ferrari lived in Italy, he reached out to him with some friendly suggestions. Apparently, Enzo wasn't willing to receive feedback from a lowly tractor mechanic and was insulted by the notion altogether. Ferrari's response to Lamborghini was abrupt and harsh, leaving Ferruccio very upset. In fact, he was so upset that he decided at that moment that (because success is the best revenge) he would build a sports car company that would supercede the Ferrari product.

The rest is history, and the rivalry exists to this day. If you take a moment to think about these events, you'll see exactly how the Avenger Drive operates. Typically, something happens, or someone does something that isn't received well by another person, and they make it their mission to prove them wrong or show them up.

Leaders who share this motivation with you are Rudolf Dassler (Puma shoes), James Dyson, and Ferruccio Lamborghini.

True North

Whether it's time to acknowledge a major change in values or shine the spotlight on what already is, your prize awaits you. When you embrace your real Firebox, expect the steam engine to pick up speed. Some people (team, clients, partners) will choose to get off on your refueling stop, but many more will get on board. The remaining crew on the ship will dig in deeper and be more committed than ever.

In times like these, it is necessary to know True North. Once you do, your organization will start to emanate your Firebox. Greatness cannot be fabricated; it can only be uncovered with a pickaxe made of vision and a shovel of determination. Hold up your Firebox high and proud. The world needs to see it.

We need to see you.

Matt Brauning

About the Author

Matt Brauning is a former writer for *Forbes*, a two-time best-selling author, and host of the top-charting Apple podcast "The Driven Entrepreneur," and syndicated on 16 AM/FM stations coast to coast.

He filmed in the movie *The Journey* with Brian Tracy and Bob Proctor, and you've seen him all over morning television on *ABC, CBS, NBC,* and *FOX*.

Matt has shared his message at places like The Harvard Club, McAfee, New York Life, NASDAQ, and the United States Air Force Academy.

He is an avid motorcycle rider, church leader, and rock climber and resides in Grand Rapids, Michigan with his amazing wife Lola and awesome son Valiant.

Contacts

The Driven Entrepreneur Podcast: Mattbrauningpodcast.com

Take the Firebox quiz: Fireboxbook.com

Follow on social media…
> *Facebook*: @mattbrauning
> *Instagram*: @mattbrauning
> *Youtube*: www.Youtube.com/mattbrauning

Appreciation and Gratitude

Michelle Jones
Life Purpose Coach and Manifestation Queen, Australia

"Be gentle with yourself because life is about the journey,
not the destination."
~ Michelle Jones

I woke up this Sunday afternoon, knowing rising from the ashes is not going to be an easy journey. Changing my mindset from a negative, overbearing one to a positive, accepting one will be a big challenge. Yes, Mish, this journey of life was empowering not only for my self-esteem but to regain my identity, an ongoing process I truly believe. Progression, not perfection, is a great mindset to have. It makes the journey of life not so hard.

The Journey

Success leaves clues. Yes, you heard of that right. What is success for you, I ask? Growing up, my mother was and will always be my greatest role model. She was a force to reckon with a charming, gentle heart of gold. Yes, God does create human beings like this. We just have to believe in ourselves. Believing in yourself is something we all have in us. Our deepest soul-searching answers lie here.

Being and taking up the role of a woman, friend, sister, wife, mom, daughter, somewhere, the sole purpose of why we were created gets lost. Behind a smile, we all have some kind of pain. Crying is not weak. For me, personally, crying is letting go of what has past. Let it flow, sister! Crying is knowing the lessons learned. Crying in these situations does not make you weak. Crying is feeling the pain your heart has. The heart will always go on. Listen to its rhythm. Is it in sync with your soul's calling or, as I call it, it's melody – your true self, your true calling, your true being.

Your true self-identity, your power, your success, your hopes, your

61

dreams, your accomplishments, your passions, your trials, your rejections, your true essence of being – Yes! This is the sweetest mystery of life. You'll get to know all about it in my upcoming book soon.

I am Michelle, born in a small town named Cuttack in incredible India. I am the youngest of four siblings. Trust me when I say I can write a book ,or even a series of books, about all the memories we had together – the good, bad, and of course, the ugly. Now in different parts of this amazing globe, that's life, right? We are still connected with that everlasting bond, which I know as unconditional love.

Siblings' love is just something special and different. My momma was a widow, and I lost my father when I was only nine years old. I barely had the opportunity to have a father-figure in my life growing up, but from what I remember of him, he was a special man, and I had the privilege to call him my Dad. It was hard growing up without a father-figure, I have to admit, but you know what? My mum did an amazing job. She was my shadow. I must say I was her shadow until death did us part, and I strongly believe that she is now here, always there to give me the strength, strength to move on, the strength to carry on, the strength to have and to hold.

Growing up, I was conditioned to always be my best. This has created the perfectionist in me. I found this very hard at times to deal with. It has created a fear of rejection. What am I talking about is how trying to be perfect can create rejections. You see, having no middle ground to fall back on was very testing for me growing up as a teenager myself. It was you either failed or excelled. The insecurities and fear of rejections, of not be valued for your achievements, took root here.

The Turning Point

The day I remember was August 22nd, 2016, the day before my mom's death anniversary. I knew in my heart that this is it. Be you fearful, or be you vulnerable, you must show up wholeheartedly and accomplish, or what I call, "manifest your dreams." Those dreams when you were a child, and before you were a mom. I wanted to be a scientist, politician, doctor – whatever I wanted to be, I had no barriers or restrictions to hold me back. What has changed?

Nothing! We are all energy, right? So let's go with the flow. Joining the business was a dream come true. Seeing empowering women, moms doing this made me think, *If she can, so can I*. Michelle was born again to give this one last go or not, I will give it a go as many times I need to, always ready for the best and ready to overcome the challenges along the way. I truly believe from the bottom of my heart. Life has trials and tribulations, but changing your mindset from it being a struggle to something you accept as a challenge. Watch how you will grow, baby! I know it! You will shine brightly. Challenge accepted! Let's do it! But, action is the key.

'When life gives you lemons, make lemonade'. I heard that saying growing up by my mother. But mom, I have to say, I have the right amount of balance of sugar and salt, and it's perfect! Just the way I like it.

Let get this over and done with. That said, I'm talking about the four years of inner work. This should be a walk in the park, right? It's more like a run in the opposite direction.

All dressed up in my best clothes, makeup, hair done, because I was told be visible in order to grow your business. I will come to the lessons learned soon. It took a whole night of no sleep, not knowing how to juggle a *Facebook Live* session and manage my children's routine.

I got on live. What did I do? I had no agenda, but just wanted to be seen. And you know what? I attracted exactly that, a total disaster. People who show up only because it is on their to-do list, half-heartedly, and who like everything for free. What you focus on expands, and I, my friend, was subconsciously attracting exactly what I wanted. The only thing was this was not my true purpose.

Lessons learned, I am still not very comfortable going live but have accepted the fact I have a great voice, and I am a work in progress, which you will all read about In my upcoming project, *Sweet Mystery of Life*.

The father of our children and I migrated to Australia 16 years ago with two black suitcases and $250 dollars. He was my worst critic, and I take it as feedback as I get to grow as an individual. So, thank you, Mr Jones, for 20 years of amazing memories together and creating three amazing babies together, but guess what? It didn't work out together with us! I release you with love in my heart. The healing is gonna be a long one, and I got to do it alone. Don't walk in front of me; I may not follow. Don't walk behind me; I may not lead. Walk beside me and just be my friend. I believe we can create opportunities if we are ready to close the wrong doors and look to open others. We should always be ready to take that leap of faith in the right direction.

This move gave us the opportunity to live in beautiful, sunny Perth, then we moved to the most livable city, beautiful Melbourne, where we now living separated! Growing up, I was always surrounded by books, one of the perks of being my mother's daughter.

You see, my mom was in charge of the library at the school. I went to St Joseph's Girls high school. To this date, she is known as 'Library Miss'. I am sure growing up, some of you loved Noddy, Nancy Drew, or the Famous Five, and I can't forget the Barbara Cartland romantic books in my teens. Books have played and are still playing a major role in my life I am living. You see, when we are busy being wife, mom, and the other roles in our lives, we forget nourishing our souls. For me it is with a book.

After having my son five years ago, I went through a depression. I just couldn't understand what was going on. It was at this time when I woke up, got dressed, and headed to our local library. I went straight to the personal development section as if someone was guiding me to get there. My eyes fell on this book. It was out on the shelf, and I read it. The book was *You Can Create an Exceptional Life* by Louise Hay and Cheryl Richardson. Reading this book has changed my life forever. I truly believe our thoughts create thing. I have swapped the negative self-talk for empowering thoughts. I never feel alone when I am with a book. Thus, my journey with books truly began again.

I always take out time to read, and it truly nourishes my mind and soul. I am a Wellness Advocate. My passion is to educate people about the powerful benefits of using essential oils. I always believe prevention is better than cure. Essential oils are the gifts of our Mother Earth, and I will continue to pursue what's pure.

The truth will set you free!

Keys lessons and Words of Wisdom

1. Attitude

My attitude never to give up is my superpower.
It's hard, but hey, at least I know it in my heart, I did not give up
I would love to share something from the bottom of my heart. When I got this amazing opportunity to collaborate with this powerful project, I was like super excited, grateful beyond something I have never felt before, but it sure boosts my self-esteem. I did have the questions come up like how can I write so well like others, but you know there is only one of me in this entire universe, so I write from my bottom of my heart and hope you will love it too.

My Dream of writing has come true in 2020, the year of awakening for me personally...

- Awakening to my emotions;

- Awakening to my voice;

- Awakening to setting up boundaries to vibrate with the highest vibration at all times. I can feel this energy now;

- Awakening to my soul's purpose to serve the greater good.

I thank my Lord and this wonderful universe for creating me, for recognising that I am a vessel to give back my gifts, my achievements, my lessons learnt, my triumphs, my vulnerabilities, and above all, my Unconditional Love .

2. No Comparisons

Comparison is the weapon of destruction. The day you decide that you were created for a divine purpose, you will rise, my sister. Now is your time. Be humble always. There were times I've had just $5 to feed myself, and I've also had $200 to go out to eat. I've had a house full of food, and at times, I didn't have any. I've been in stores cashing out with no worries, and I've also had to add it up and put things back on the shelf.

We all have highs and lows in life, some certainly more than others, but we're all just trying to make it.

No one is better than anyone else, and my heart is sad for those who think that they are better. No matter how big your house is, how new your car is, or how much money sits in your bank account, we all bleed red and eventually fade from this Earth. Be kind to others. We all are here to serve our oversized egos and know that not everyone has the same heart as you.

3. Appreciation and Gratitude

Have you ever experienced a gentle warmth around your heart when someone appreciates you or when you express your appreciation and gratitude for others? This is one of the amazing properties of the powerful human emotion of appreciation.

You are the greatest manifestor of your dreams .Just as the caterpillar thought it died, but yet she grew wings and transformed into a beautiful butterfly.

Light and love always,

About the Author

Hey! I am **Michelle Jones**, an empowering women and mom to my three beautiful children. I was born in the small town of Cuttack in Incredible India. I am now a Life Purpose Coach and Manifestation Queen currently living in Melbourne Australia .

Writing is my passion, and I believe words creates opportunities for everyone. Empowering women to rise to the highest vibrations is what I am all about. I am a Wellness Advocate and know prevention is better than cure. In my spare time I take out for myself every day, I love reading personal development books, dancing, and singing at the top of my voice.

The Power of Networking

Naomi Beverly, M.A., M.Ed.
Transformational Coach, USA

*"Don't wait to be great. Don't ask permission. Decide what
it means to you, and be great starting NOW!"*
~ Naomi Beverly

The Meltdown

Remember what you promised yourself when you and your ENTIRE family almost died in that crash with the 18-wheeler in July 2020? Remember what you said your 'why' was? When are you going to make your first *TikTok* and begin incorporating what you learned from the Virtual Business Summit we attended?" my business partners inquired during one of our daily prospect calls.

"I'm going to make it this week. I'm watching my *YouTube* tutorial and learning how to make my first video!" I replied.

The truth was that I was so extremely nervous about creating a *Tik Tok* video. I came up with the "tutorial" idea as a masquerade to conceal my deepest trepidations. While I don't mind public speaking and doing LIVE social media videos, I froze in fear at the idea of trying to be "relevant" or "trendy" to use *TikTok* for attraction marketing. The idea was frightening and made me nauseous.

However, I understood that it was something I needed to do to massively impact the number of people who would hear about my businesses. A *TikTok* video is one of the most effective and most influential strategies to use with attraction marketing. It's many times more effective than putting still images on social media feeds. When it is done right, it can beat engagement on all other social media platforms. This attracts warm leads to you and makes them want to know more about you and what you offer.

But how would I be able to get over my fears? What mindset shifts did I need to make to "do something that I've never done before to get results that I've never gotten?" I wonder if you can relate to my thoughts and self-talk because that's exactly what I was thinking and what I was telling myself. With my current, fear-based mindset, the blocks were so gigantic that they were paralyzing me from moving confidently in the direction of my goals, desires, and dream life.

I remembered giving my first live *Facebook* video at the request of my business coach in our cohort's warmup activities during the first week of April 2020. We were tasked with sharing our new business with the world on our *Facebook* page in a PUBLIC post! What!? Was she bananas? I never even really put anything personal on my FB page, let alone told people that I don't know a lot about a new business I was creating.

I recall my throat tightening and my voice pitching up higher, as it does when I am nervous. I couldn't talk clearly. I wasn't breathing normally; it was rapid and shallow. My hands were shaking quite a bit, so the video was shaky as well. I paid attention as others created their first live videos and posted them on the Facebook platform, and then decided to give it a go!

I grabbed my phone, found the app, pressed the "LIVE" button, and put on my best smile. I followed all of the advice I had been given – pretend like I am talking to a friend, check my camera angles, try to connect with the audience, and just be my authentic self.

Several minutes after the live video, my business coach and cohort responded via the comments. Overall, they said, "You did great! You didn't appear nervous at all!" If ANYONE knew..., they all knew how panicky and fearful I was during that first-ever live video. The good thing was that I got over my fear that day and learned the power that getting better at one little aspect of how I do business can have a massive impact.

I experienced similar apprehension and angst as I prepared and researched before my first *TikTok* video on social media. I really did find a *YouTube* video tutorial. Then, I found a blog that broke down the "whys" and "hows," the algorithms, and hashtags. I saw others in my organization create their first videos that received THOUSANDS of LIKES and reached out for help and tips. I was nervous, timid, sweating, but determined to take this step forward into 2021 with my FIRST *TIK TOK* video posted to promote my business!

In addition to that, my business partners challenged me to do *TikTok* videos and share them to my other social media platforms or *Facebook* LIVE videos themselves for 30 days straight. The purpose was to increase engagement and build trust and consistency more quickly. *What?! What would I say? Moreover, who would care to watch my video?* I thought to myself. It was daunting, but I was going to make it happen.

The fear was crippling me. Overthinking and the idea of wanting it to be perfect were major stumbling blocks and obstacles stopping me! I have a saying: "Completely done and imperfect is INFINITELY more powerful than perfect but incomplete." I was going to have to fail forward if need be!

The Turning Point

My turning point came on December 15, 2020.

I was meditating, visualizing, and manifesting my vision board and goals for 2021. I realized just how much I had gone through from 2018 to 2020 — a whirlwind courtship but abusive marriage; a pregnancy that I spent alone; surviving infidelity; moving from my hometown of 30 years to escape; and starting over with my young children and infant; surviving a devastating multi-vehicle hit-and-run accident with an 18-wheeler in which all of my children were injured, one severely; starting a new job and a new career; finishing up my second master's degree; starting not one but TWO LLCs – one to help others who have survived trauma rebuild their lives; filing and finalizing a divorce; completing my Mental Health Peer Counselor training with the Georgia Mental Health Consumer Network; becoming a #1 Bestselling Author; securing my first keynote speaker engagement; and last but not least, investing in my first business coach.

I had recently reengaged with my network marketing company and completed a PHENOMENAL training session. I was refocused, refreshed, renewed, and rededicated to living my BEST life, NOW! I realized that I had mentally shifted from being in breakdown to realizing my breakthrough. I had moved from trauma to transmuting the pain into purpose and power. Emotionally, spiritually, physically, and mentally, I was ready to transcend into the BEST version of myself. I was aligning my vibration and intentions with my goals and deepest desires. THE most amazing people began showing up in my life. It was clear that my dreams were all in my line of sight. I just had to do my part. I learned that I had to embrace that the Internet and social media are critical in my success as a businesswoman in the 21st century. I was going to have to create that first *TikTok*!

In addition to mastering *TikTok,* there was a whole formula full of strategies and sound business principles that I want to share with you that I learned from some amazing, wise, and successful mentors, teachers, and coaches. I was given the opportunity to take inventory of my current levels of performance and compare them against what the most successful network marketers are doing to sustain their success.

There are five essential elements that must be mastered to have lasting results. They are: Leadership, Presenting, Duplication, Social Media, And Personal Growth.

Principle #1: Leadership

My network marketing mentors have earned millions in their business over 20+ years in the business. They've led hundreds of others to making between $50,000 to $1 million+ per year. They understand that leaders have to understand not only their business, but their people as well. Great leaders know how to allocate their time and focus. It is a fact that in the business of network marketing, not everyone should receive the same amount of time or type of focus.

A great leader is going to invest the most time in those who are coachable, hungry, and willing. They have to know how much to challenge each person and give assignments that grow and stretch their team without overwhelming them. Some people need more coaching than others. Some need help with mindset but are professionals at social media. A great leader can leverage the strengths of not only his or her personal team and network but the strengths of others in their sphere of influence.

Principle #2: Presenting

Those who desire to sharpen their presenting skills should understand several foundational components to being a powerful presenter: the art of the personal story; 3rd-party validation; opportunity presentation; onboarding new team members; and training your team. A great presenter knows the business, they know the products, and they know how to close.

One of my favorite storytellers in the world is Lisa Nichols. She talks about how to craft a compelling story that allows others to connect with you on a personal level and leads them to trust you, which ultimately may lead to them wanting to conduct business with you. In addition to your personal story and success, using the success of others as 3rd-party validation gives more credibility to your presentation. It's a "secret weapon" you can use to help close the deal. It's why testimonials and mentioning your business or opportunity has been featured in trusted media can sway a consumer's mind, leading them to want to complete a transaction with you or invest in your opportunity.

What I love best about my company is that everyone who is introduced to the service and/or the business gets to listen to the top earners and the most successful people first. That doesn't mean the people who have been in the business the longest, either! Some people are born leaders, take the opportunity, and fly immediately! Listening to their opportunity presentation or watching them onboard and train new team members can be even more inspirational to others who are new. This is because newer people can possibly relate to a person who was in their shoes a year ago easier than the story of someone who has two decades in the business.

Principle #3: Duplication

"Radical Duplication" is a term network marketing great Eric Worre uses to describe how to grow and scale a network marketing business. He uses an acronym "ACTS" to describe how to achieve it. A is for assignments, C is for campaigns, T is for tools, and S is for systems.

Assignments are the step-by-step actions that are going to get a person from where they are to where they need to be. Campaigns are the special one-time or recurring CTAs or "calls to action" that, for example, re-energize the team or take advantage of a season (like a holiday promotion) or circumstance (qualification of a special event or incentive). Tools are what specific strategies or skills people need to achieve their goals and level up. A business itself is a large system made up of various other, smaller systems. Systems are the core elements of a business. Systems help a business run. Processes are steps taken to make systems run efficiently. Knowing the systems of a business well and learning the processes certainly allows a person to radically duplicate their success. Even better, joining a strong TEAM who is already doing this then plugging your prospects into the system is an even better strategy for radical duplication.

Principle #4: Social Media

As we have already discussed, social media is a fantastic tool to use for attraction marketing and growing a business. Currently, three platforms have proven to return the most "bang for your buck" – *Facebook, Instagram,* and *TikTok.* Each platform has specific strategies to learn to maximize one's success. However, for all platforms, it's important to take an inventory of your profile and optimize it. Learn about organic- and paid-lead generation tactics. Connecting with popular influencers is a strategy to widen your personal network of followers and "friends," as is using hashtags strategically, intentionally, and effectively. Using trending music/songs and modeling content that is already successful are other ways to increase your personal success.

Principle #5: Personal Growth and Mindset

One of the most important components of success is, of course, personal growth and mindset. If we cannot lead ourselves, we cannot lead others well. If we don't know how to coach, it will be difficult to build a team, then lead that team to success. We must ourselves be coachable, hungry, and willing. Personal development includes getting better in many areas, including time management, emotional intelligence, resiliency, listening, mindset, skills acquisition, public speaking, getting along with ourselves and others, facing fear, and developing strong habits. This can be done by finding mentors and coaches, attending seminars and training, reading books, and studying the lives, habits, and mindsets of other successful people. Work toward getting 1% better every day and watch how much progress you make!

I'm really fortunate that I have made it to see my 40th birthday, that I have a loving family, a great career, a thriving business, and all the peace, love, joy, and abundance that my heart can stand. It makes up for all of the challenging times. And, I'm happy to report that I finally DID make that first *TikTok*, after all! It ended up being enjoyable. Let go of your fear and do that ONE intentional thing each day that will make you get "1% better each day," as my mentors Darnell Self and Alistair Edwards say.

Power Summary

Let's recap some of the key points in this chapter:

1. Fill in the blank. Completely done and imperfect is INFINITELY more powerful than _____..

2. What are the five essential elements that the most successful network marketers are doing to sustain their success?

3. What do you think the impact on your business or life will be when you choose to get 1% better each day?

Success Actions

Here are three actions that you can complete to help you realize success:

1. Post your first *Tik Tok* video (or *Facebook Live* or *InstaStory*) on social media if you haven't done it yet. Challenge yourself to do it for 30 days, even if it's just for one minute at a time.

2. Write down and say your mantra/declaration about letting completion. Example: "Completely done and imperfect is INFINITELY more powerful than perfect but incomplete."

3. Take ONE action today that's going to help you get 1% better than you were yesterday. What could go wrong? Instead of thinking that, think, "What could go RIGHT?" Write down that one action and just have fun doing it!! Smile, laugh, play...and GROW!

"You've got a finite amount of time to fulfill your purpose.
Face the fears, learn the lessons, seek out the skills,
conquer with confidence, and do the things necessary so
you can pat your own self on the back and say, 'Self...,
Well DONE!'"
~ Naomi Beverly, M.A., M.Ed.

With much love and gratitude,

Naomi Beverly

About the Author

Naomi Beverly is a transformational coach, #1 Amazon International Bestselling author, Mental Health Peer Support Specialist, and singer from the United States of America.

Her company, Naomi Beverly Coaching LLC, helps people rebuild their lives after trauma one-on-one or in a supportive group community using self-publishing for self-care plus other tools and strategies. Her favorite types of books are those dealing with Social Emotional Learning.

Naomi Beverly holds a B.A. in Videoing, Telecommunications, and Mass Media, an M.A. in Education, and an M.Ed. in Instructional Design.

During her free time, she enjoys dancing, yoga, meditation, working out, eating well, and being in nature. Naomi is the mother of four amazing children, two of whom have self-published and are in business for themselves. Their company is Sound Design and Development LLC.

Contacts

Email: naomi@naomibeverlycoaching.com

Schedule a 15-minute discovery call or book sessions at:
www.calendly.com/coachnaomi

Facebook: Facebook Community Trauma Survivors: Self-publishing as self-care:
https://www.facebook.com/groups/selfpublishselfcare

Purchase the book *Birth (Volume II): Stories of Birth, Renewal, and Birthing a New Earth* in the USA at:
https://www.amazon.com/dp/B08K86H76V

You Can Overcome Anything Despite the Barriers in Life

Nor Suhir
Certified Social Media Strategists and Business Coach, Singapore

*There is **only one me**. It's my **own** journey. What makes me **different**? I **decide** the ending.*
~ Nor Suhir

The Meltdown

December 2015 is a month I will never forget. I suffered my first stroke. Two weeks later, I suffered a second stroke which caused my retina to detach. After that incident, from one eye, I saw complete darkness, while the other was just a blur. A few months later, I suffered yet another stroke. This was the start of a four-year journey that changed my life forever. I became an infant again. I had to learn how to talk because my speech was slurred. I had to learn how to eat – how to chew and swallow – so that whatever I consumed did not end up choking me instead. I had to learn how to climb stairs, how to hold a pen, pick up coins, and other small items. The list goes on and on.

Doctors were unable to immediately reattach my retina because of the stroke, so I had to learn to do all those things with almost zero vision. When they finally managed to operate on my eye, life decided it was not done with me. That same retina detached again after a few weeks. I had to go through a series of eye surgeries just to get my vision back.

The physical therapy from the stroke was exhausting. I wanted to throw in the towel several times. I used to be a cheerful and outgoing person who was always active. As a consultant and coach, my days were filled with meetings and appointments with clients. Networking, training and coaching sessions filled my daily schedule. Engaging with an audience on stage felt like second nature, but with the blink of an eye, I had to be confined to a bed. I did not have the strength to move around on my own, even if I used a walking stick. Someone had to accompany me everywhere I went. I lost count of the number of times I visited the hospital in those four years. It became a second home.

It did not take long before I became sad and depressed. I felt ashamed to appear in public. I became reserved and timid but did what I could to keep my feelings to myself and not show it to my family because I knew they were feeling stressed-out too. My son had to sacrifice his studies by taking two semesters off to take care of me. It made him lose his scholarship.

I have always been the backbone of the company. The multiple strokes caused my business to go into pause mode. We were unable to bring in new clients because of my inability to move around. One-by-one, members of my team had to leave because we did not have enough money to pay them. We had to be prudent since there was barely any income. I was not afraid of shutting the company down if I had to because I believed that when my health got better, I could build it back up. But, what did make me fearful was the possibility that my health would not improve, that I would lose my eyesight forever and not be able to speak normally since the stroke attacks affected the parts of the brain that controlled speech. If I was unable to see and speak, how could I rebuild my business?

Fortunately, I was soon able to move around with the help and support of my family. At that point, I knew I had to muster the courage to meet people. I cannot run a business hiding at home, life must go on.

Having to put up a happy front to clients was a challenge. Pretending I could see them even when all I saw were only shades of grey was nerve-wracking. I gave the excuse that I was having a bad, sore throat during business meetings when people could not understand me. I was afraid that they would find out that my speech was slurred and that I had forgotten what I had wanted to say in the middle of a conversation. What would happen if my clients found out about my health issues? Would they terminate the contract? Would they still trust me to finish the job? I believed that, deep down, I was still the same person with the same capabilities, especially when it came to business strategy and helping my clients get new customers. It was only my physical state that was affected, but would they continue to believe in me? We needed the money. There was a lot of uncertainty, anxiety and stress, and it was crippling.

I had to start believing that I could do the job again!

There were so many negative thoughts. I experienced anxiety attacks and extreme stress. I could not explain how I felt. I wanted to break down and cry after every meeting because I was not able to convey what I had in mind effectively. It felt as if my mind was working faster than my ability to speak.

One day, my husband and son had a heart-to-heart talk with me. They advised me to stop focusing on the handicap. They reassured me that I am good at what I do, despite the disabilities. I had to draw my focus back on why I started the business and what makes me happy – my passion for helping others grow their business.

Worrying about the things that I have no control over will not make me happy. It will not help me, my family, or my clients. At that point, I sat down and reflected on everything that had happened. I had to make a decision – either I sink with self-pity or swim to the shore and pick myself back up.

The Turning Point

It took me a good three years to pick myself back up. I was able to walk on my own without a walking stick. I was able to talk without slurring, even though I had to speak slower. I was able to visit the hospital on my own. Even though my vision remained greyish, I was able to see the outline of a body, so I knew I would not bump into anyone anymore.

On September 2019, I finally got my full vision back. I cannot explain how happy and relieved I was when I saw the blue sky, the greenery, read a car plate, read the signboards, and saw people's faces. It took a good ten minutes for everything to sink in. That feeling remains indescribable. Then, on 11 September, my birthday, I made a vow to rebuild my business. I vowed to grow it bigger than ever. I made a resolution to focus on automation so that my business and my clients' businesses will continue not only to survive but also to thrive in any situation or economy.

I spread out my business risk by diversifying my investments in other companies. I started putting my skills, knowledge, and training materials onto online platforms. I shared my health issues with my mentor, Ms Tina Williams from Bold Angels. She understood what I went through because she was also a stroke survivor. But most importantly, she was a friend when I needed one the most and was someone with whom I could resonate. With Tina's help, I started to rebuild my business. She guided me on how to handle my current situation and urged me to go back to the basics of what she taught me when I first became a Certified Social Media Strategist.

I went back to the drawing board with my husband and son and began strategizing my business goals. I mustered the courage to go out and talk to potential clients face-to-face. Yes, I stuttered. Yes, I stumbled. Yes, I had to pause frequently throughout the meetings and presentations. Even though I felt like I had failed and fell flat on my face after each meeting and presentation, I kept persevering. I kept falling, but I also kept getting back up. I have always believed that how one gets up is crucial. I was relentless in the effort I put into my work. I kept telling myself repeatedly, *I must do it for my family. I am great. I am a fighter. I attract business everywhere I go.*

The Impact

We received an email from a potential client that I did a presentation to a year prior. She saw the transformation that I achieved for a neighbouring business when I was their coach. I was able to achieve in less than a year what she had been trying to do for two years. The client gave us the job, and it boosted my confidence by 1,000,000%!

I started working diligently with the client, strategizing and transforming the business through automation and implementing internal systems. I helped introduce new products and services that were scalable and have now part of their core offerings and have grown to become their main revenue stream. The best part – it was all achieved in less than two years.

At the same time, I also started working on transforming my own business and bringing it into the online space. I created new online training courses to help businesses digitize. I mustered the courage to record videos, conduct *Facebook LIVE* sessions and dug deep into building systems that help to completely automate businesses' sales funnels. The 2020 pandemic situation motivated me to help more businesses acquire new customers through automation. I found mentors that could help guide me in crafting my 'Unlocking Multiple 6-Figure Business Formula'. I worked on my system, started building automation software, and taught the psychological secrets to being a leader with a vision and mission. I focused on helping others believe in their identity and use it to find new opportunities. Pouring all of my efforts into helping others gave me a new perspective on my own business.

A year later, I mustered the courage to apply everything that I had learned in a two-month-long campaign with a client. It was the only client I had at that point. It was either sink or swim. After two months, the business generated almost 700 new customers and $70,000 in additional sales. But, I knew one success was not enough. I approached another potential client and took a big risk – I told them that they did not have to pay me unless I was successful because I wanted to do a proof-of-concept. It was an industry that has a lot of restrictions due to the nature of the business. I needed to not only prove to the client that my system worked, but also prove to myself that I could do it. To cut the story short, I helped the business generate close to 140 new customers within a two-month period. It boosted my self-confidence, and I knew I found my jackpot.

But that was still not enough. I spent more time working on a system that was duplicable and scalable. A system that could be implemented with minimal effort, irrespective of the level of skill of the person implementing it.

Today, as I am writing this, I am happy to share that my system is currently being implemented by my clients.

The Belief Will Set You to Help Others Too

I help business owners acquire the skills and develop the systems needed to unlock their multiple six-figure business and thrive in any economy. I am a 'Rainmaker' in the small business world with the abilities to identify ideal customers for any business. For those who share the same dream but have yet to realize it, I believe I can help them finally become a 'Rainmaker'. Not only will they have the ability to build a multiple six-figure business but they will also be empowered to help others too.

In August 2020, I launched my own automation platform, *ChatEngaged*, which has helped automate 90% of the work that I do with my clients. The interesting part about using my platform and system is that it has helped my clients be 'Rainmakers' themselves. It was no longer just about me, it was also about them helping themselves and others.

Key Lessons and Words of Wisdom

Giving up is not an option. My new journey of transformation has only just begun. It is as if I have been reborn. The chapters of my life prior to my stroke has long ended. My focus should be in the present and in the possibilities that the future holds. The tide will turn at the right place and time.

You will never know what you might find when you take the first step. Trust yourself. You are a leader with a vision and mission to help others. You just need to train your mind to default towards success.

There will never be a proverbial, perfect time to start. You need to just take that first step. You will fall, but what matters is that you get up again. You will make mistakes, but you will overcome them. It was because I took my first step that I was able to achieve the things that I thought was impossible before. The wheels are now in motion, and it is not going to stop any time soon.

Within one year of my full recovery, I was able to launch my own customer-generating system and positioned myself as an authority, expert, and influencer in my field. Now, I help entrepreneurs build a 'Rainmaker' for their business and others through my free masterclass:

http://norsuhir.com/weeklymasterclass

All these would not have been possible if I had not taken that first step.

After going through the process, I have listed the key lessons learned in my path to success, below. Give yourself permission to be you. Control your identity because it is 100%-based on your action.

Wisdom #1 – Believe in Yourself

Through this journey, from the day I suffered my first stroke until now, I came to realize that my self-belief was what led me to turn my life around. It has helped me change my life and my environment. I am me. I am unique. I create my own reality by asking who I am going to be, who I want to be in my future reality, and build an emotional connection with myself and my goals.

Wisdom #2 – Be a Leader

This is **me**. I need to focus on my direction, brand, and impact on my audience. Build a proven framework that is clear, scalable, and generates predictable recurring cash flow that is easily duplicable. As a leader, I must help others be successful as it is never just about me alone.

Identify my 'why' and what I can do to step things up, and influence and impact my audience positively. There are many out there who teach what I teach. But I know that there is **only one me**, and that makes me special. I use this to position myself and focus on filling the gaps in my target audiences' needs.

Wisdom #3 – Strong Backend System

Systems are an important piece that's missing in most businesses. It is a formula that guides your actions and business decisions in order for you to achieve your goals and objectives.

One of my business' backend systems is my ACC formula – Attract,

Connect, Convert. The main purpose of the ACC formula is having conversations with my audience that will eventually convert. My objective when applying it is to generate one appointment a day consistently.

Every business needs a strong backend system. People out there focus too much on putting out content. Content alone will not bring me paying customers if I have a weak or non-existent system that ties all my marketing activities into a cohesive flow. When I develop and implement my backend system, my business changes tremendously.

Your backend system can help you build relationships with your audience.

Wisdom #4 – Take Action

For a journey to begin, you need to take the first step. However, how far you are willing to go is determined by your motivation to succeed. It all starts with your attitude, a clear vision and that courageous first step. If I can do it, there is no reason why you cannot.

The Rewards

I am grateful that now I am able to move around independently and talk to people, especially strangers, without stuttering. I am grateful that I am able to help my clients build their businesses. I am grateful that my business that had to stall due to my poor health is now slowly but surely coming back up again.

My journey has only just begun, and I have no intention of stopping any time soon. I am extending my hand to you to share your story and to come and walk our respective journeys together. I know some of you have to swim hard to keep your heads above the water, but I want to be there for you. You never know, your rainbow might just be around the corner.

Recently, I was invited to be the President of the Hawkerentrepreneur Chapter at International Business Federation Singapore in order to help local F&B businesses digitalize. I also finally launched my own backend system *Messenger* bot, *Chatengaged*. Now, I teach business owners all around the world to be 'Rainmakers' and unlock their multiple six-figure and thrive in any economy. Be a 'Feedompreneur'!

http://norsuhir.com/weeklymasterclass

You are a 'Freedompreneur' when you have people chasing to buy from you because you have a proven framework that delivers insane results. You have built a brand that impacts others because your Magnetic Message resonates with others.

Power Summary

Giving up is not an option.

My unique message is what connects me with my audience. It gives me the ability to help others.

For my business to attain a multiple six-figure income and have a constant stream of new leads, I need to set up a strong backend system.

Success Actions

1. Your online business relies on three key aspects – Traffic, your Sales Conversion Process, and your High-Perceived Value Offer.

2. Focus on selling the outcome. People buy based on emotions and use logic to justify their actions.

3. Set up your duplicable and scalable backend system that aligns your audience into your acquisition system. The main focus of this backend system is to help your audience solve their most immediate problem.

"I do not live to make my presence noticed. I am unique.
My story is unique. My journey is unique. I want my
absence to be felt because I live for a cause!"
~ Nor Suhir

With Love and Blessings. Be Healthy

Nor Suhir

About the Author

Nor Suhir is a stroke survivor, Certified Social Media Strategist, Business Coach, and author of the upcoming book, *You Can Overcome Anything Despite the Barriers in Life*. She is also the President of the Hawkerentrepreneur Chapter at International Business Federation, Singapore, helping local food and beverage businesses digitalize, and recently launched her own *Messenger* automation application, *ChatEngaged*.

Contacts

You Can Overcome Anything Despite the Barriers in Life:

http://norsuhir.com

ChatEngaged: http://chatengaged.com

Life Is All About Choices

Priyanka Mukherjee
Law of Attraction Coach and Business Consultant, Scotland, UK

"Self-love is not selfish; you cannot truly love another until you know how to love yourself."
~Priyanka Mukherjee

When Life Crashes

It was a Saturday morning. I had cried myself to sleep last night. It seemed like my life had fallen apart. My relationship was over, and the previous night I had spent a few hours trying to convince him to stay. I was not enjoying my work either. The travel and traffic added to my frustration. I was left with no friends, and I felt I had no one to talk to. I felt so terrible for myself that I wanted my life to end.

I woke up and went to freshen up. I looked in the mirror, and I couldn't recognize the person I was seeing. Who was she? Where was the Priya I had known? She used to be a happy, carefree, and confident person. The person I saw in the mirror was someone who took pity on herself, had lost all her self-esteem, and was weak. I fell on the ground, crying, praying to God to help me out. I begged the universe to help me get out of this life and change myself.

A few days had passed, and I was trying to cope with life and the situation. I became desperate to change my life and started looking for ways to change it. I had read the book *The Secret* before, and it came to me that the book said your life is a reflection of your thoughts and the way you feel about everything in your life. It was at that moment that I realized that my every thought and feeling had become so negative. I didn't feel good about myself, my job, the traffic, the city, the people, ...and the list was so long. I could think of 100 things that I didn't like easily but hardly anything that I liked. Everything became so clear to me at that very moment.

The Turning Point

I started focusing on and analysing everything about my life. I remembered that the time when life was good and everything worked for me, and it was all because I had faith in myself. I was carefree. I didn't worry about anything. I didn't force anything to happen. I was so focused on myself that everything else was aligning. When gradually, I tried controlling the outcome and wanted things to be in a certain way, I started being unfulfilled and unhappy. I had started associating my happiness with the outcome of other people's behaviours. I was so desperate for other people to change and treat me 'right' that I forgot to set my boundaries. They kept pushing my boundaries, and I kept giving them chances, hoping for them to change. They kept mistreating me, and I let them. In turn, I kept feeling as if I was not good enough. It was at that moment that I realized that I let other people decide my worth for me. I was so busy looking for validation that I forgot to love myself.

From that moment, the sole purpose of my life became to change myself. I decided to bring the focus of my life back to myself, but I did not know where or how to start. I re-read the book *The Secret*. This time when I read it, I truly understood the meaning of the book. For anything to change in your life, the only place to start is with yourself. When you change what's inside you, the outside automatically starts changing.

I created a routine for myself, which I decided to follow for at least the next 30 days of my life since it is said it takes a minimum of 30 days to create a new habit. And one thing that became clear in my mind was that creating this new version of me wasn't going to be easy. It was going to need all my dedication and commitment and all of my time since I was trying to create something totally new – new thoughts, new beliefs, new self-image, a new mindset, and a new perception towards life. But, my desperation to make myself better was so much that I was ready to do whatever it takes.

The Self Commitment

I started with the process of self-healing. It was challenging in the beginning, but I kept on doing it every single day, no matter how difficult it seemed. I started my day at 5 a.m. with these activities:

The 1st Step was practicing gratitude.

I began my days by thanking the universe for everything I had at that very moment in my life. I forced my mind to think about everything good in my life. I started focusing on every detail, no matter how big or small they were. When you are grateful for everything, you have you attract more. The Law of Attraction states you bring in your life what you focus on. So, I started focusing on everything that I had, and I started to realize the more I focused on the positive, the more number of things I could think of to be grateful for. Every single day by practicing gratitude, I healed my life more and more because my mind gradually started focusing on the good things in my life, and my perception about my life changed.

The 2nd Step was taking care of was my mind.

The mind is a very powerful tool, and as it is said, it can be your best friend or your worst enemy. It all is depending on what you feed your mind with. Most of us think that our thoughts and feelings run on autopilot mode, and we do not have any control over them. But the biggest truth is we all have control over the way we want to think and feel. I started practicing meditation every single day, and it turned out to be the biggest blessing in my life. Meditation helped me calm my mind and have control over what I wanted to focus on during the day and the way I wanted to feel about myself. Mastering your mind is an art, and the one who has been able to achieve that is a true artist. We are the creators of our life, and we are doing that every day through our thoughts. The day I started taking responsibility for my thoughts, feelings, and actions, my life changed. I no longer depended on others for my happiness. I created my own happiness, and it was wonderful.

The 3rd Step I took was to develop my self-confidence.

Self-confidence is the key to living a peaceful and successful life. When you become enough for yourself, and the outer world doesn't affect you in any way, you have reached a dangerous level of freedom. It wasn't easy in the beginning. I started by setting small goals for myself. No matter what my mind told me, I forced myself to do what I had set for myself. By achieving small goals every day and be able to conquer my mind, my self-confidence started developing. I made a list of things I would do every day and made sure I completed them every day. Initially, I had to force myself but gradually, they became my habit and came with ease, and my days felt incomplete without them. Within a few weeks, I could feel the difference within me. My faith in my own self was rebuilding. I started believing in myself, and my will power started getting stronger. I started believing that I can achieve whatever I set my mind to. I started being mindful, and gradually with my newfound self-confidence, I could control my thoughts and handle any situations that came in life.

When you start believing in yourself, the current circumstances don't matter. Your faith in yourself helps you look beyond what's visible to the naked eyes. Self-confidence enables you to connect with your instincts and develop faith in the unknown. It's one of the greatest gifts you can give to yourself.

The 4th Step was I started taking care of my body.

I started pampering myself. I became careful about the food I ate. Just like the mind needs to be fed positivity to develop a positive attitude, your body needs proper food to nourish itself. The food you intake has a direct impact on your energy field and your mind. I started working out regularly and fell in love with my body. Everything which I found was imperfect about myself, I fell in love with. I loved my body equally as I loved my mind. I did everything out of love for myself. And with time and love, my body started changing, and my face started glowing to the extent that people started noticing and asking me what I have been doing differently. Some people said they couldn't recognize me anymore. There was something very different about me now.

The 5th Step was the commitment to myself.

The final step and the most important step, without which I wouldn't have been able to change my life at all, was my utter self-dedication and commitment to myself. No matter what happened, I continued doing what I had set my intention to. No two days or even two seconds are the same. There were lots of moments when it felt it would be easier to stay in my comfort zone or take a break, but I knew that what I am doing right now, my future self will thank me for that. I continued doing it every single day, even if that meant forcing myself to do it. A few days I had to force myself a little bit more, and a few days, it came easy. But the repetition of the same process every day helps you incorporate it as a habit.

Those days that I dedicated to just myself turned out to be the best days of my life. The outcome was unbelievable. Once I had healed myself and started believing in myself, everything around me changed. I realized my worth and started setting my boundaries with people. I realized the people who once I thought I couldn't live without were the ones who I did not need in my life at all. Once I changed my relationship with myself, my relationship with others started changing. I started enjoying my work; I made new friends, and the traffic started getting smoother every day. The way you perceive anything in life, whether it is a situation or people, is a reflection of how you feel about yourself. The day you change your relationship with yourself, everything else starts changing.

The New Me

So many people ask me why is the law of attraction not working for them. I say the law of attraction is working all the time for every single person. The only difference is the ones who truly manifest their desires are the ones who change themselves, and not the ones who try to change others. The moment you start focusing on the situation and wish for the situation to change, you are creating the same pattern again and again. The situation is what it is supposed to be. The only thing that needs to change is your perception, your attitude, and your feelings about the situation, and that happens when you look within and not outside.

Accept whatever is right in front of you. Acceptance is the first step to change. Do not let external factors determine how you feel about yourself. Remember, the way someone perceives you is a reflection of themselves, and it has got nothing to do with you. You are only who you truly believe yourself to be. Change your own self-image in your own eyes and experience the entire world change right in front of you. Protect your own energies always.

Remember, many people will want you, but only a few will deserve you. Be brave to cut people out of your life. It is ultimately your life, and you are the only one who must live it. So, hire some people and fire other people, and live life regret-free. There are no mistakes, only experiences, and make sure to learn from those experiences.

It's your life. Don't let anyone tell you what you are and what you are not capable of. If you believe in yourself, everything is possible. It is your life, and you are the only one creating it, so create the life that you want to live.

Trust the process and trust yourself, and everything else will fall in place.

Success Actions

1. Be hungry for self-development. There is nothing that you can't achieve when you put your heart to something.

2. Get into a routine. To change your old pattern of life you need to create a new one. The new you can be created when you work on yourself every single day and create a new pattern.

3. Love yourself the most. Remember you attract what you become, and you become what you feel. So, make sure you love yourself unconditionally. When your inside heals the outside starts to shine.

4. Learn to set your boundaries with people. Everyone will try to push your limits and try to get their way but set your limits with everyone. Don't let anyone bring you down. Be brave enough to cut people out of your life. This is your life you are the only one living it.

5. Learn to respect yourself. Do not ever compromise on self-respect. People treat you the way you treat yourself. You reflect what you feel about yourself. Your outer world is a reflection of your inner self. If you want something to change then look inside of yourself.

"Set Some Goals…
Stay quiet about them…
Smash the hell out of them…
Clap your god dam self…"
~Priyanka Mukherjee

Lots of Love and Happiness,

Priyanka

About the Author

Priyanka Mukherjee is a Law of Attraction Coach and Business Consultant working with Accenture, and she lives in Glasgow, Scotland in the United Kingdom. She helps people who want to transform their lives and create a better one for themselves. She runs her own *YouTube* channel and a *Podcast* explaining the Law of Attraction and how to manifest the best life for yourself.

She also conducts online sessions where she guides people on how to heal themselves and change their lives.

Contacts

YouTube:
https://www.youtube.com/channel/UCuqhyBlsCxBkoh4y7ZhMIvw

Find Your Voice

Razia Naqvi-Jukes
Personal Brand Photographer, UK

*'It's not what you are that holds you back, it's what you
think you are not.'*
~ Razia Naqvi-Jukes

The Meltdown

Imposter syndrome was one of the biggest struggles I have faced all my life. So, when I changed my career from being a teacher to a photographer, the perceptual thoughts that have sat with me all my life came flooding back. *I'm not a real photographer. I'm a teacher. My degree is in teaching, not photography. I'm not creative enough.* My internal thoughts would circle in my mind continuously, and they would follow me on every shoot in the early days.

Thinking back, I feel I've always struggled with being an imposter. I remember being in class in primary school, and the teacher using me as an example of being a model student. I wasn't smart, not in the traditional way. School was a struggle. But somehow, I was getting away with being in the top sets. I found it so hard to keep up with the teacher and focus for the whole lesson. As long as I could make it look like I was listening and quietly doing my work, I could pull off being a model student. It was the mid-80s, and teachers didn't have the same accountability as they have now. Somehow, I got away with it until a simple class test revealed that I belonged to the bottom sets. The shame was deep and cutting. It was soul-destroying. I remember the shock on my classmates' faces when they realised I didn't belong in the top sets. Dyslexia didn't have a voice then. You were either stupid or intelligent. There were no other labels. Despite my external smiles, deep down, I felt unworthy and not good enough.

I took these feelings of unworthiness with me into my adult life. They echoed in everything I did. Lack of self-worth is so crippling. It influences every decision you make. In my case, it affected the decisions I made when choosing the subjects I studied. I didn't select the subjects I loved; I chose subjects I thought I could do easily. I decided to be a primary school teacher instead of a secondary school teacher because primary school has got to be easier, right? (No offence intended to primary school teachers.) I soon learnt primary school teaching wasn't the more comfortable option. There is a big difference between loving something and choosing safer options. I always played it safe.

The Turning Point

But playing it safe stopped being an option when my husband left me. In 2007, I was a single mum with three very young children. I was depressed, shocked, and overwhelmed for the first six months of his leaving. I was unable to do anything other than the simplest, most basic tasks. I'd manage to get the children to school and then sleep until school pick up time. I lacked energy and the enthusiasm to do anything. I knew I had to find a way out of the terrible spiral of pain that crippled me. I had to be a better mother for the sake of my children.

Something made me pick up the camera and start photographing my children. I started documenting their everyday life. It was beautiful watching and observing them – the way they played, the way they interacted with one another. I observed the light. I developed ways of anticipating the moment, and mostly I noticed something magical unfolding.

I started to notice the beauty in the everyday. Observing life through the lens helped me focus on the beauty that existed already in my life. The feelings of hurt and unworthiness started to change to feelings of gratitude. The truth is, the beauty in my life was always there. I just had to stop and see it. I remember reading a quote at the time that resonated with me.

'It's not what you look at that matters, it's what you see.'
~ Henry David Thoreau

I was seeing for the first time through the lens of gratitude.

I Found My Voice

Alongside this, my photography just got better and better. My kids were young toddlers, and they never stayed in one place for long. Acting fast and knowing I didn't have enough time to get the shot meant I had to move quickly. I was flourishing, growing, and for the first time in my life, I had a voice. Photography gave me a voice. It allowed me to put all my feelings of hurt into my work and turn that pain into something beautiful. It allowed me to express myself in a way I couldn't before. It was almost like speaking without words. My images encapsulated everything I felt, and that felt liberating. I was free. Free because I was heard. Free because I could express myself. Free because I was redefining my newly found self-worth from purely being able to express myself.

I shone, and I could feel it! There was a newfound confidence in me that all could see.

Other mums soon picked up the uniqueness in my work, and after an exhibition of my work, I was asked to photograph a wedding.

The feelings of unworthiness started to make their way to the surface. *I'm going to mess up. I only have one chance to get it right. People are going to know I'm not a real photographer. Photographing a wedding is going to expose the holes in my work. What if the light is too low? What if I mess up the key shots? I won't get the chance to do them again.*

The Breakthrough

I remember when I got my first wedding booking. I spent two weeks running through the wedding timeline in my head and thinking of all the different scenarios that could happen on the wedding day. I rehearsed where I would stand for each shot, and I envisioned how each image would look. The run-up to the wedding was so scary. The fear of being an imposter reared its ugly head again.

But, I knew I had to do it and breakthrough. Pulling out wasn't an option. I just had to stop focusing on my fear and start focusing on what I wanted to accomplish. I had to focus on what the end result would look like. I wanted to achieve beautiful, storytelling images that my lovely bride and groom would look upon and relive. I wanted to create the same beauty that healed me, but for others to enjoy. What I wanted was to give my couple a legacy that they could leave to their children and their children's children, a glimpse of whom they once were. I wanted to capture each couple uniquely and authentically. I found myself doing it again. I was given a voice, but this time my vision and lens became a voice to tell other people's stories.

So, with all the fear of failure in my heart, I left early to shoot the wedding. From the first click of my shutter, something amazing happened. My anxiety disappeared, and I fell into a surreal zone where everything slowed down. I was able to see images before they happened, just as I had visualised. I was using my feelings of empathy to synch in with the emotions surrounding me to anticipate other people's reactions. By doing so, I was able to foresee the moment and be at the right place at the right time.

That night, I loaded my images to the computer with much anticipation. *Did I get the shots I needed?* Well, the pictures I got were amazing! I was so proud of them, and I had proven to myself that I could achieve for others what I did for myself.

Unexpected Results

My '**why**' was now bigger than my fear. The very thing that lifted me was now my purpose for others. Had I stopped with my fear, I wouldn't have achieved the breakthrough for my brand, and the best was yet to come!

I refined my style and my brand. My brand stood for images with emotion, beautiful light, and connection. I got better and better with each wedding. And then, I was noticed by a *YouTuber* and lifestyle influencer Lily Pebbles. She loved my work. I remember Lily saying how she went through so many photographers' portfolios and loved the softness and emotion in my work. It spoke to her. I was so nervous about this wedding as it was a high-profile wedding. *Had I bitten off more than I could chew? Was I going to get found out?* If I don't do a good job, it could ruin my career. The same fears crept back into my mind, but I had to remind myself to focus on the outcome I wanted and not my fear. If I focus on the fear, it will stop me from moving forward. By focusing on the outcome and visualising it, it would become my reality. This magic equation has never let me down.

Her wedding was a success! Lily texted me straight away after seeing her gallery of pictures. She told me she was 'blown away by them'! I went on to photograph the wedding of another influencer, Samantha Maria. Sam booked me after seeing Lily Pebbles' pictures. Their pictures were published in magazines. They were getting anywhere from 60,000 to 100,000 Likes on *Instagram* every time they were used. I noticed that in every subsequent wedding I photographed after these two, I was seen as a celebrity by the brides I photographed. My brand had moved to the next level.

Understanding the power of my brand and how it helped me stand out, my mentor then encouraged me to focus on female entrepreneurs. A spark in me aligned with this idea because my **why** is giving a voice to others, making one feel visible when they have felt lost. I would be telling their brand story through my pictures, so they felt heard and understood. I photographed my clients in the most beautiful, authentic way I possibly could. *Wow! Why hadn't I thought of this before?* Photographing entrepreneurs was the perfect direction to add to my work.

By working with entrepreneurs, I was able to see how empowering branding shoots were. A personal branding shoot takes a person and gives their message a voice. It brings their vision to life as something tangible. And once they had a voice, these women were invincible. Helping women project their message gives me so much joy.

I have since photographed many wonderful women.

My Roots

I am so blessed to be able to do what I love, and I didn't think this could be possible for me. I was brought up to believe academia was the only route worth perusing.

I grew up on a council estate in Birmingham, England, in the '70s and '80s. My father had come to the UK to follow his passion for doing a PhD in the UK. He was a scientist, and he desired to get a British degree. I was the eldest of four children with three younger brothers. As my father was a student for much of my childhood, my mother worked to make ends meet. A working mother and a father who was studying meant that I had to step up and look after my brothers from a very young age. From as young as seven, I took on the responsibilities of getting myself and my brothers off to school every morning and tidy up the house before my mum returned from a busy day at work. It sounds harsh, but I didn't know any different.

I had an eclectic upbringing. I grew up on a mostly racist council estate, which crushed my self-worth. But I managed to muddle through this by finding a small group of friends that accepted me for me. I had friends that were local to the estate but also had family friends that were doctors and lawyers. This taught me to be able to talk to all people from all walks of life. I could chat with the locals on the estate as well as prominent CEOs and people of power with confidence.

I'm very grateful for this journey because although it was tough when I look back, it taught me some fundamental lessons.

It taught me that people are people, and we must be kind and respect one another.

It taught me resilience. Despite it being a racist environment, as long as I restricted myself to certain people, I could minimise the effect on me.

It taught me branding from a young age. Stick to your values, and you will attract your tribe. Not all the people on the estate were racist. Your value doesn't decrease by someone else's inability to see your worth! I had to align myself with people who accepted me.

Lastly, it taught me how to visualise. Despite my challenges academically, I always imagined myself in a better situation, and that life was going to be better. I did get to university, something my teachers didn't think was possible for me. Visualisation, coupled with action, works! I honestly don't think I would be where I am now without these experiences.

The Wisdom and Lessons Learned

Having travelled this journey to success, I list below the key lessons I've learned on the way. I hope that you'll find strength from my wisdom because you're **worthy** of success too!

#1 Have Your Voice

The wisdom I have learnt from my experience is there is something empowering about having a voice. Especially if it's your voice echoing your values. There is something freeing about being heard. Find a way in which you can put your emotions into something that helps you feel visible and heard. Being authentic and having your message heard and understood is how to step into your **power**. You won't step into your power by trying to be like others. That's when your message becomes lost amongst the sea of sameness, and that's when you lose you. If my values and my personal experience did not clearly define my brand, then I may never have been seen or chosen by Lily Pebbles. There are thousands of photographers out there, but she chose me!

#2 Investing in Your Brand

If you are in business or thinking of starting a business, then investing in your brand is a must! If you want to get high-ticket clients, you have to think big. People choose **you** because of the promise you have made in your brand. What is your promise? My promise is beautiful, authentic, storytelling images full of emotion, light, and connection. When someone chooses to book me, they know what they are getting. They have already brought into my brand and my promise. Investing in your brand is the best investment you can do because it aligns you to your ideal client. Done correctly, your brand does all the selling for you.

#3 A Big Why

Your 'why' has to be bigger than your fear! This is a big one. The thing is I didn't want to create generic images of women holding coffee cups sitting by a computer. I wanted to capture these women authentically. I wanted to capture their 'why', their personality, their personal stamp of uniqueness. I wanted to capture their soul and tell their story. It had to shine through in my images. I had to give these women a voice because I knew how it saved me and propelled me forward. So, my '**why**' was now bigger than my fear.

#4 What You Focus on Expands

Stop focusing on what you think you are <u>not,</u> and start focusing on what you can become. See the result. Visualise it until it becomes real in your head and then do it. I found by seeing it first in my mind's eye made it possible! It helped me <u>feel</u> that it could be possible. The truth is 'anything' I have ever visualised has always materialised. It's so important to focus on the thing you want to achieve and <u>not</u> your fear. If I had focused on the negative, then I wouldn't have been able to work through my blocks. The way forward is to focus on the positive. What you focus on becomes your reality!

The Reward

I am so grateful for the brand I have created. I have continued to photograph some amazing women from powerful CEOs of companies to high-profile influencers and coaches. I have been invited to be interviewed on *TedEd* and *Podcasts*. My photographs have been published in high-profile magazines and mainstream newspapers. I've become a best-selling author. I love empowering women with a voice and spreading their message.

Let go of your fear by focusing on the outcome you want in your life and don't overthink things. Like the brand Nike said in one of their campaigns,

'Just do it'!

Success Actions

Here are four things you can do right now.

1. Define your 'why'. It has to move you. It has to be bigger than your fear.
2. Write down your goal – your big dream.
3. Visualise it!
4. Do one thing today that will move you closer to your goal. Don't overthink it!

> „Be humble. Not knowing something does not make you a
> fraud, it makes you a student!"
> ~ Maria Forleo

You've got this!

Much love,

Razia xx

About the Author

Razia Naqvi-Jukes is a personal brand photographer, filmmaker, and consultant. She lives in London, UK, with her husband and three children.

She loves helping women define their brand and help project its message. Her methods have helped elevate her brand and the brand of others. She has worked with famous influencers and entrepreneurs. She is a best-selling author of *She Made It Happen* and has been featured in *TedEd*: The Impact of your images on social media.

Contacts

Join My Free Mini-course: The Art of The Six Figure Brand Accelerator.
https://www.facebook.com/groups/692877941444939

Website: https://razia.photography/personal-brand-photographer

Instagram: https://www.instagram.com/raziajukesphoto/

Facebook: https://www.facebook.com/razia.naqvijukes/

Linkedin: https://www.linkedin.com/in/razia-naqvi-jukes-5037631b0/

TedEd: The Impact of Your Images on Social Media
https://ed.ted.com/on/GoBIIdsY?fbclid=IwAR234UkPjJIrwXLDztPIIPVpFmK
dHjgtjgIAGdW3YyAOQVTwo9SZsJLkwPs

Poor or Rich?

The Question that Sparked the Fun and Friendly Way to Track Financial Health

Sheri Muz
Entrepreneur, Malaysia

"The dictionary is the only place where SUCCESS comes before WORK."
~Vince Lombardi

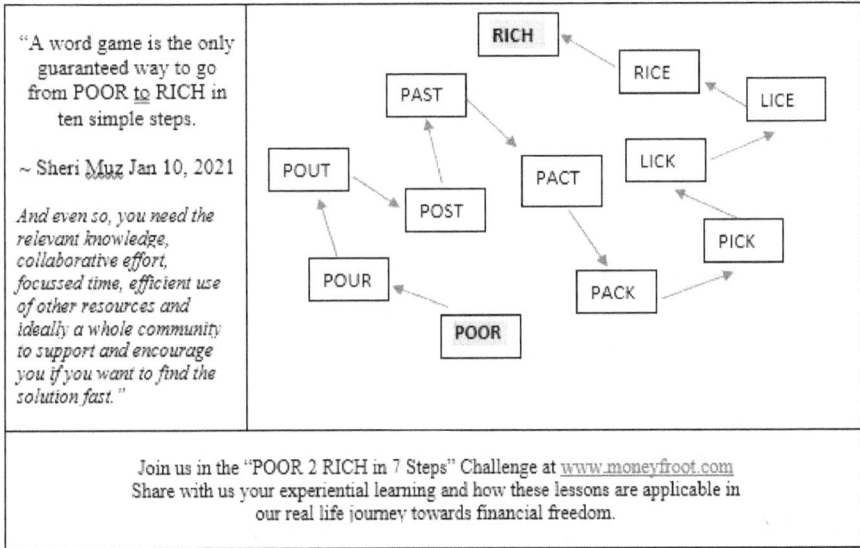

"A word game is the only guaranteed way to go from POOR to RICH in ten simple steps.

~ Sheri Muz Jan 10, 2021

And even so, you need the relevant knowledge, collaborative effort, focussed time, efficient use of other resources and ideally a whole community to support and encourage you if you want to find the solution fast."

Join us in the "POOR 2 RICH in 7 Steps" Challenge at www.moneyfroot.com
Share with us your experiential learning and how these lessons are applicable in our real life journey towards financial freedom.

The following is my story of how I came up with MoneyFroot, a fun and friendly personal money management system and why it is only now that I am sharing this knowledge with the outside world. Join me in the kick-off and development of the MoneyFrooters community, where we support each other in our journey toward financial freedom. Whether you are an employee, solopreneur, an entrepreneur with staff, or anywhere in between, you will get value from this.

"Mama, are we poor or rich?" asked my three-year-old out of nowhere. This was somewhere in 2008.

I was stumped!

To say we were poor wasn't quite right. Although I have no income and was staying with a friend and repaying her kindness by doing the dishes and keeping the house clean, I still have a comfortable nest egg even after more than three years of unemployment. We had no issues with shelter, food or safety and had easy access to books and transportation.

To say we were rich wasn't right either. Though I didn't hesitate to buy books and food, I wasn't as "fancy-free" with my personal development books and programs as before. I found myself a lot more calculative with my budget since my nest egg couldn't probably last another two years at the rate I was going.

I was still going through one alternative treatment after another for my medical condition, which modern medicine had given up on, and going back to a regular 9-to-5 wasn't an option.

But even if I could say that we were rich or poor, how do I explain balance sheet and income statement, assets and liabilities to a child who was just beginning to understand colors and shapes? She was just memorizing her 1 to 10, with reading limited to "A is for Apple" and "B is for Ball".

Besides, my financial literacy wasn't a lot more advanced. The only reason I had a nest egg to fall back on was accidental and not planned~ I had been single, had a good-paying job and a low-key lifestyle, not much commitment and saved whatever was left over after expenses. Though the nest egg was a lifesaver at that point, I found out later that this way was the wrong way to save. But more on that later!

After a few eye-blinks along with absolute silence on my end, my daughter ran away to play with her friends, leaving me stumped as to how to answer her question.

And to be honest, by that time, I was also asking myself the same thing! Was I poor or rich? How do I know for sure? What is the definition of "poor" or "rich"? And at the end of the day, does it matter?

This incident led me on a journey of discovery, lasting a few years, by trial and error. I was looking for something simple enough that even a 3-year-old could understand, that any number-phobic adult can relate to and that any parent can use to explain to their young children. But more importantly, if my experience was anything to go by, I was looking for something for an adult who should know better but still got into financial difficulty.

Over the next few years, I developed a reasonably workable answer based on my own research and others' experiences, tweaking bits and pieces as and when necessary. I used this system to dig myself out of the financial hole which I found myself in when my nest egg finally ran out.

My findings showed that the age-old wealth principles have stayed the same over the ages, from Babylonian times to the present if George Clarkson's story in his book the *Richest Man In Babylon* is anything to go by. And in addition to Biblical and Quranic guidelines, the contents in modern personal finance books and blogs are based on the same concepts as well.

Apart from Robert Kiyosaki's re-definition of "assets" being something that brings money out of your pocket and "liabilities" being something that takes money out of your pocket, there really isn't anything new nor earth-shattering, no magic wand that provides a different path towards financial freedom.

So, I worked at giving different meanings to the same financial items, making it easier to understand and remember, which helped me stay on the right financial path. Hopefully, the same will work for you.

Take, for example, my savings behaviour. Before, I had savings only because I had excess money at the end of the month. But during my "sabbatical" I didn't save because there was no excess at the end of the month. I decided to define two different types of saving: pre-expense and post-expense. Once I had decided on exactly what they meant, I became a pre-expense saver. Before, I didn't follow the conventional advice of "Pay Yourself First", i.e. to put aside a portion of your income before spending the rest.

In my system, pre-expenses savings are live seeds that one day could sprout and give me more fruits. Post-expenses savings are like cooked or dead seeds, suitable only for consumption and not income expansion. Suddenly, even saving one small live seed makes sense to me.

Why Now? Why Not Before?

By the time I finished giving different meanings to debts, assets, liabilities, compounded interest, credit card balances and other financial ratios, my financial statement looked like my daughter's color book – a seven-part cross-section of a fruit, bamboo stems and pictures of colorful fruits!

At a glance I knew my financial health by looking at the number of seeds, the color of the pulp, the thickness of the skin and the shape of the fruit. I celebrated changing from a strawberry to a dragon fruit, while keeping in mind my medium-term target of being a banana. When I went shopping the vision of the strawberry vs the banana kept me on budget.

It was weird to say the least and was probably what held me back from sharing with anyone.

So why now? There wasn't any specific day or big event, no thunderbolt or light bulb popping, no whack on the head that gave me the nerve to share. It was probably a combination of small things, most likely triggered by a year of early retirement as well as the Covid situation.

The voice in my head said "Hey, it is now or never. 60 is just around the corner." I am not getting younger, and if I don't share it will be such a waste. Sooner or later, I will be nothing but worm's food.

I decided to go for it, to give different meanings to all the excuses that had held me back. And to trust my gut feel.

Thinking about it now, I realised that when I made truly major decisions in my life, I shortlisted with logic but selected on gut feel. The decision would pop out of the blue with no rhyme or reason.

For example, when I quit my job and planned to recuperate and be back at work in 6 months, I instead adopted a baby girl! The planned six months' recovery turned into six years as I wanted to be around as much as possible in my daughter's first six years.

Adopting and becoming a single mother was the most illogical thing to do. I was already in my early 40's, set in my ways and usually couldn't hold a baby without having the baby crying its head off. I couldn't really take care of myself, let alone a baby, as I was perpetually on pain-killers after a major operation. My friend who said I was crazy to quit at 42 told me that it would be difficult to get a good job after six months away from the corporate world, let alone the six years I had in mind.

But things worked out well with my flesh-and-blood baby, and I am confident the same will happen with my online baby. Starting www.MoneyFroot.com feels like another "out of the blue" decision, another baby whose cries I would probably be at a loss to manage.

I cannot pinpoint when I stopped seeing obstacles and started having different meanings for my excuses. Perhaps the following quote from a program I attended more than 20 years ago that just popped up in my head helped that change.

> "Obstacles are mirages in the eyes of winners yet are brick walls in the hands of losers".
>
> Jez Izman Izaidin
> "Awareness Before Change" Personal Devt Program

Essentially, it means to choose what I want my reality to be. I guess the years of this personal development program is finally bearing fruits!

The Truth that Set Me Free

So, I see mirages and choose what I want my reality to be. I no longer see brick walls when I think about my fears, baggage and excuses.

OLD MEANING	NEW MEANING
▪ How can I equate a balance sheet and income statement of the Wealth, Middle Class/ Rich and Poor with types of fruits like strawberries, grapes, and rambutans? ▪ This may be ok to me, but isn't it too whacky for others, especially the highly educated ones? ▪ Wouldn't it be insulting to the average adult to be explained to in a language that's fit for a pre-schooler? ▪ How can I be sure I am not doing more harm than good?	▪ There is no right or wrong way, appropriate or otherwise, valid or not. This is just my life experience I am sharing, which may be useful and relevant to some and not others. ▪ Expect both brickbats and bouquets. As for acceptance, some people will, some people won't. I shall not let these concerns hinder my journey. ▪ It worked for me. It should work for some of the others as well and not harm anyone.

A boy told his mom that he wanted to quite school. When his mom asked him what he was going to do with just two years of school, he said, "Mom, I am going to teach the first graders."

OLD MEANING	NEW MEANING
▪ Who am I to sell such an idea or system? Though I have a college degree, it wasn't in finance, accounting, or economy. And I have no professional experience in personal finance.	▪ If someone with two years of education can teach the first graders, I can share my system with anyone who is open to learning.
▪ I have done business presentations and in-house training, but that is a far cry from training strangers who would be paying out of their pocket. What if I couldn't deliver?	▪ MoneyFroot is my way of managing my financial health. This isn't rocket science or brain surgery. I will be fine.
▪ How do I get this done without a big budget? With almost zero experience with social media and technical stuff, how steep is my learning curve going to be? Can I afford the coaches, software, and system needed to get this off the ground successful?	▪ Just start and figure something out as we go along. Let's see what the interest is out there first.

What Now?

Once I made the decision to start www.MoneyFroot.com, it's amazing how peaceful and "anchored" it feels. Not the laidback type of rest nor "don't-have-to-do-anything" mindset, but a sense of **Just Do It!**, manage the hurdles and do the minimum viable first.

The super-duper costly automation will have to wait. I believe the solutions and answers will appear at the right time. In endeavors like this, logic will only carry me so far. I need to believe and depend on the magic of the Universe's accounting system.

I mean, how could anyone believe that the concept of "give before you get" works? But at one level or another we do believe in the magic of the Universe's accounting. We believe that

- The more you give, the more you get, no matter how small the contribution.

- The more you teach, the more you learn, no matter how insignificant the lesson.

- The more you smile, the happier you feel, no matter how bad the external situation.

- The more steps or actions you make, the bigger and faster you will move, no matter how small and wobbly the first steps.

Illogical, but true…

Let's band together on this financial freedom journey using a friendly and unconventional tracking system to first contribute to others, and see what comes back to you. I am focusing on employees who have an income, as I see them as the first line of defense to ensure a community's financial well-being. COVID-12 has more than shown us that. "To help the poor, first make sure you are not poor yourself."

And before we can get to where we want to go, we have to know where we are now. Financial freedom journeys start with knowing what the current financial health is. But an income statement and balance sheet in its numerical format is intimidating for most people, even those with college degrees. Hence MoneyFroot's format of translating the numbers into colors and shapes.

www.moneyfroot.com was initially intended to help employees understand personal financial literacy in a fun and friendly way, while helping them be better in their career with any income-generating activities not interfering with their day job. However, our business model is also applicable to employees planning for retirement or other forms of exit, whether in the short or long term, as well as employees who have started something on the side or are now business owners.

For more info on "MoneyFroot: The Fun and Friendly Guide to Personal Money Management", please visit www.moneyfroot.com or contact me at sherimuz@moneyfroot.com.

Words of Wisdom

Visit the website above to find out more about the practical aspects of these wisdoms:

Wisdom #1: Learn from your and others' experience the positives and negatives, as they are all challenges to see how much we have fulfilled our "job description" as human beings.

Wisdom #2: The teacher shouldn't matter if the student is ready. The beggar can teach us how not to be poor or broke.

Wisdom #3: The best humans among us are those who contribute to others on a consistent basis, no matter how small – from something as simple as a smile, a good word, to best wishes for others' well-being.

Wisdom #4: Know that you are already wealthy. But until you are truly grateful for what has been given, you will never feel wealthy.

Wisdom #5: Start giving until you are rich; don't wait until you are rich.

Wisdom #6: Spend less than you earn until a time comes when you can earn more than you spend.

> "Don't buy a car that is more attractive than you!"
>
> ~ Sheri Muz

About the Author

Sheri Muz (Sherifah Muznizah) has more than 20 years in HR, with a focus on compensation-related matters, industrial relations, and general HR administration. In her years of working, she developed salary structures during her consulting and freelancing years and at the companies where she worked. She managed and oversaw the processes of allocating bonuses and how to give salary increases.

But yet in those many years, Sheri Muz has never seen or known, until recently, any companies that have provided financial literacy knowledge to help employees manage their income.

Simultaneously, she has seen how financial difficulties, even with high-salaried employees, interfered with employees' work performance. On many occasions, she has been approached by employees asking about promotion opportunities as a way to get a higher salary to solve the problem of not having enough. And almost without fail, on an annual basis when bonuses were paid, there were unhappy faces as the quantum received wasn't enough to cover the debts or new year expenses.

Sheri grew up in Malaysia with four siblings. Her father died during a tour of duty when she was eight, leaving a single mother who had two years of pre-war education. Fortunately, her mother was very creative with income generation and prudent with money management.

Sheri holds a Bachelor of Mathematics and an MBA, both from California.

Contacts

Website: https://www.moneyfroot.com

Email: sherimuz@gmail.com or sherimuz@moneyfroot.com

Consistency Is Key

Vandee Flake
Elite Network Marketer and Entrepreneur, USA

*"You will never change your life until you change
something you do daily.
The secret of your success is found in your daily
routine."*
~ John C Maxwell

The morning I took the pregnancy test, I was ecstatic. My life was moving right along the track I had planned out in high school. I had graduated top of my class and earned a scholarship. After graduation, I had a job that paid well, and I had moved up to a manager position. My husband and I had one darling little girl and were trying for our baby number two. My husband, Sam, was working as a teacher, and we had just remodeled our home. However, the top-of-the-world feeling didn't last. One morning I woke up, bleeding. I called my doctor and went in to hear the devastating news that I had miscarried our sweet baby. Not knowing what else to do, I went to work as normal. I didn't tell my boss for a week.

Why do we, as women, push ourselves so hard to be perfect at everything? Why did I feel the stress of my job was more important than my health and my family? I realized that I had given up on my goal to work from home so I could balance my work and family.

We were able to have another baby. The pregnancy was rough, and I knew that I could not do it again and work the stressful job that I had. We had been living in a rut with work and two kids. We were not putting our marriage on our priority list, and we were barely surviving.

Becoming an Entrepreneur

It was during this overwhelming time in our life when my husband informed me that a friend invited us to a network marketing meeting. I reluctantly agreed to go but told my husband he was not to bring his wallet or credit card. Quickly, I realized that this wasn't a me-too product, and I was intrigued by the story and the science behind this. I did realize the possibilities, but I didn't let the slick-talking, out-of-town friend blow the opportunity out of proportion. After a rather quick study of the company and the science, Sam went to meet with the leaders. Finally, we decided to dip our toe in.

Now, one thing that I really dislike about the network marketing industry is false expectations are usually set. If you want to make the income of a doctor or lawyer, you know how much time and schooling that takes. If you want to be successful in any industry, you need to invest an average of 10,000 hours. However, most people are content with the 40:50 plan – work 40 hours a week, for 40 to 50 years, then retire on 40% of your paycheck. The brilliant part of network marketing, in my opinion, is the opportunity to learn from millionaires and billionaires on the techniques and strategies that they used to get to where they are. The education portion is equal to the action. The other amazing thing in this industry is you can earn while you learn. As you polish your skills, you become a better version of yourself.

You Become the Sum of the Five People You Spend the Most Time With

At my first big event, I remember a speaker sharing that you become the sum of the five people you spend the most time with. Never had a quote hit my soul with more force, and I love quotes. I sat pondering for days because I realized that, with the exception of Sam, the other four people were co-workers, who I did not want to become. I had become a version of Vandee that was worried about work, did not put in her best effort, and did not reach for her goals or dreams anymore. I had become complacent and apathetic. I feel like apathy is one of the hardest things that I struggle with. It is so easy to become distracted from our dreams and let apathy lead the way. You become the average of the five people you spend the most time with. **Pick wisely!** You choose who you listen to and learn from.

Pick wise mentors. Read or listen to authors to help you become the best version of yourself.

This realization that I was meant to do more than go to work and die, that I needed to become the best version of me that I could be, was hard to take. Realizing you are apathetic and living in a rut is a hard slap in the face. So, I began a two-pronged approach; I did two things every day.

I learned something new. Some days it was the same CD over and over again. There are so many amazing resources that you can use for personal growth. A few of my favorites include John Maxwell, Bob Proctor, Mel Robbins, Eric Worre, and many other personal development coaches.

The second was I took action.

Daily Activity

John Maxwell speaks about the importance of taking time every day to work towards your goals. He states that every day he reads, writes. and edits. People ask him, "But John, what about Christmas or your birthday?"

He responds, "Every day, I read, write, and reflect – not all day, but a little bit every day."

There is such power in daily, consistent action. Whether it is building as an entrepreneur or writing a book, daily activity consistently, over time, will have amazing results. Look at John Maxwell, he is a legend with over 25 best-selling self-help books. His courses are amazing and inspiring.

This action of daily activity wasn't easy. The simple little steps were easy to do, and they were easy to skip. It wasn't an "Ah-ha!", brilliant moment that you do once, and your life changes forever. It was the little, almost invisible, steps forward that accumulated to cause a huge change in our life.

I struggled with learning something new every day. I was busy. I worked a full-time job, often skipping breaks and lunches for work. I had two small children, and we were active in the community and our church. So, I decided that I would enroll in a mobile university. My driving time (one hour each day) became my classroom. I listened to recorded calls, bought CDs, and listened to them over and over. I remember a training where the millionaire said, "I can't sit in your car each day and motivate you." I thought, *Man, I wish he could!*

The first CD I bought was a recording of that exact speaker. I thought, *I have this now. I can have any trainer I want with me all the time.* Where can you squeeze in your learning? What about the shower or the car in the early morning? You can do it!

Decide your daily routine and schedule these training sessions into your day. If it's working out, make calls, learn more about your business, or work with clients. **<u>Schedule it!</u>**

I try to focus on four core areas of my life each day: social, mental, physical, and spiritual. One little step each day will make a huge difference. I have found that I achieve my goals faster when I put it on my calendar with a reminder. I have a bad habit of not wanting to write down little things or schedule things that don't take long, but when it's on my calendar, I realize that I do better.

Write Down Your Goals

The next inspiration that hit me right between the eyes was a learning session on goals. I felt like I didn't have any goals left. However, there was one goal that I had discarded as unattainable and unrealistic. Sitting in that class woke that goal up and brought it to the forefront of my mind and heart. I wanted to be an entrepreneur so I could work from home and raise my babies. I also decided that my "momma heart" had been cheated, and I wanted a third baby that I could raise.

My goal to have flexibility and time choice soon became the forefront of my daily activity. Number one, I had the desire. Number two, I wrote it everywhere. Funny story about this, I came home at midnight from this training, cleaned off the mirror in my room, and wrote four goals down:

1. Mom home from work

2. Baby #3

3. $10,000 checks

4. Debt Free

My daughter came in the next morning, and with her little hand on her hip, she reminded me of the rule to only draw on paper, not the mirror. We had a quick discussion on goals, and why we write our goals where we can see them. She asked if we could add Disneyland to the list. So, #5 became "Disneyland for the family" goal.

Daily Action Pays Off

After 30 months of focused learning and activity, we reached a point where we could make a change in our lives. I retired from my job the next Monday, and I found out that my goal of having our third child was coming true also. However, with the completion of this huge goal, we were able to make family time a priority. We were financially blessed to have options.

Our business expanded again with a wonderful team in Hawaii. I flew over there seven months pregnant to meet with an incredible tribe. The one thing that I didn't realize up to this point in my entrepreneurial business was the health and financial benefits were amazing, but the **friendships that have been created will change you into a better version of yourself.**

This business has introduced me to friends all over the world, people I would have never met if I hadn't become an entrepreneur! Daily action will pay off. The creation of this lifestyle did not happen immediately. Instead, it was a compound effect of daily activity.

Take Time to Rest, not Quit

After my son was born, I dived back into traveling and building my business. My adorable sidekick traveled to eleven different states, including Florida and Hawaii, before he was a year old. I created a network of women who wanted options to travel and the choice on how to raise their families. My life was incredibly blessed. Our business had doubled in size, and life was fun.

I went to an all-women's event, and I came home so excited and so sick. Everyone at the event ended up with a cold, so I didn't think much about being sick. My husband flew out to work with a team across the country, and I didn't get better. I found out that I was pregnant again. This was a high-risk pregnancy because of medical complications. I was in constant fear of losing the baby. I also had a toddler who needed me and two older children in school. We had just purchased a small pizza business that we were trying to get up and running.

In the midst of all this stress, I heard this quote, "Take time to rest, but don't quit." Sam and I re-evaluated our priorities and closed the pizza shop. We canceled travel plans and put the family as a top priority. We hired help to get through the tasks that were too overwhelming. We took the time we needed. We rested, but we did not quit. After my sweet boy was born, healthy and strong, I had to have two surgeries the next year. However, we took time to enjoy our sweet baby. When life gets overwhelming, it's okay to take time to rest, but don't quit. Don't give up on your dreams and goals because it gets hard.

Life is an Adventure – Vision Boards

On our vision board, we added several more goals: a cute little farm, travel, and adventures as a family. After our baby was born, we bought a little farm out of town. We raised cows, pigs, sheep, dogs, cats, and chickens. This presented good lessons for our kids to learn responsibility and work ethic. We also learned about keeping animals safe from hawks, crows, and coyotes. We had some sad days and some great memories. About the time that we had the little farm all situated, Sam decided it was time to move again. I was devastated for a bit, but we discussed our goals and dreams, and decided to be crazy.

We sold everything and bought an RV. We left Arizona and headed East. We realized a few things early on. Traveling full time is not like a vacation. You have to plan downtime for work, laundry, walks, school, and just to chill. After slowing down our travels, we had some incredible and crazy adventures. We enjoyed seeing friends and new places. The memories we created will last forever. We also enjoyed exploring historical sites with our kids. I could write a book just on the lessons we learned and the places we saw. We flew to Cancun for 11 days in February of 2020, and the adventure was truly memorable. We decided when we got home that we might extend our 18-month RV trip and looked at international destinations. Sam and I had traveled to Europe, the Bahamas, and Mexico, but we wanted to experience this with our children.

However, the next month, all plans were changed as COVID-19 hit. Living in an RV with four children when you couldn't even go to a playground was scary. As plans were canceled and life was changing, we re-evaluated our goals. It was curious to me that with all the beautiful places we had seen in our travels, our kids wanted to go home to be closer to family and friends. We were able to buy a home, and we are settling back into a routine. Every decision needs to be evaluated to determine if it will bring us closer to our goals or if it is just a distraction.

Three Steps to Get Back on Track

Becoming the best version of yourself is not a one time, aha! moment. It is the small daily actions that compound to change your life. "When life hits you, and you feel like staying in bed under the covers, curled up in the fetal position. What do you do?"

I've been there many times in my journey. One of my dear friends and mentors, Seth Mulder, who created the concept of CEO, *Creating Entrepreneurs Online*, shared this, and it felt like the perfect thing to share with you. Here are three steps to get you back on track.

First, stop and count your blessings. Don't just say "I'm grateful." Really stop to count the blessings you have in your life. List them out, name them one by one. I try to add three blessings to my gratitude chart every day. When I hit the down times, I realized that I have usually slacked off in my gratitude list.

The second step is to reconnect to your vision. What's your vision, and why do you want to succeed? Reconnect to your vision. I highly recommend a vision board or goal sheet somewhere visible that you'll see every day.

The third step is to take action. Action each day creates a compound effect that will change your life.

Apathy vs. Happiness

I've realized that happiness is a choice. We cannot control everything that happens to us, but we can control how we react. I've found a few things that help me find daily happiness. These little things each day will make a big difference: gratitude, outside time, exercise, sleep, drinking enough water, and eating right. Then add your daily activity to achieve your visions and goals. These ways are how you choose happiness.

Being an entrepreneur is a daily battle against naysayers and your own insecurities. However, daily activity will change your life.

Yes, I can do it, and **yes, you can also.**

Power Summary

1. You become the average of the five people you spend the most time with. **Pick wisely!**

2. Decide your daily routine and schedule them into your day.

3. Be specific on your gratitude list and your goals.

Success Actions

1. Spend at least 15 minutes a day with one of your mentors. Learn and grow every single day.

2. Take time each day for you to visualize your goals. Take a walk, meditate, but think about your goals.

3. Spend time working for your goals. Decide what action needs taken every single day and schedule it into your calendar.

Live with intention. Walk to the edge. Listen hard. Practice wellness. Play with abandon. Laugh. Choose with no regret. Do what you love. Live as if this is all there is."

Vandee Flake

~ Mary Anne Roadacher-Hershey

Best wishes.

Vandee

Vandee Flake

About the Author

Vandee Flake is a native Arizonian. She graduated from Arizona State University in 2003, followed by a nine-year career in marketing. However, once she became a mom, she realized that this wasn't the career path that would give her the time flexibility to be a modern-day mother.

Vandee and her husband started their journey ten years ago in network marketing. This has been the answer to their prayers for better health and more time flexibility for their family. Vandee is passionate about helping entrepreneurs and encouraging women live their own dreams. She has built a successful business and loves to help others.

Vandee and her family traveled full time in an RV with their children for 18 months. This may have been the best or the craziest decision for them. COVID-19 has changed their plans for now.

Vandee's goal is to connect with other people who are looking for better health, finances, or more time freedom for themselves and their families.

Contacts

Instagram: www.instagram.com/travelingflakes

Facebook (Business): www.facebook.com/happinessjellybeans

Facebook (Personal): https://www.facebook.com/vandee.flake

Email: vflake@gmail.com

Critical Courage to Freedom

Veronica Crystal Young
Leadership – Resilience – Change Expert, USA

"Your past does not define you; your today does."
~ Veronica Crystal Young

I am 12.

I think my arms are going to be pulled out of their sockets as I am dragged out to the old camper that is parked in our front driveway. His hands are so big, clenched hard over my tiny fingers, and I think my hand is going to break. The smell of cheap cologne is overpowering, like he had drenched himself in it to cover up the shame and pain of what he is about to do. He pulls me inside and up to the bed on top of the cab. I am not resisting because no one can know about this. It's my fault, and I'm so ashamed and scared. I stare up at the camper ceiling and pray that no one will hear me if I let out a scream. I don't feel any pain because I am numb. Seeing the only way to survive the pain, I leave my body to float up to the corner of the camper, disconnected from the horror of what is happening and to disassociate from who I really am and this moment. And all I can think is, what did I do to deserve this?

I am 8.

We have the perfect family. My mom met my dad in the Korean War while he was stationed in Germany, and he brought her to this country when she was 18 years old. By 24, she had all four of us kids, my three brothers and me.

My three brothers and I have so much fun! I do everything the boys do, and I am a bit of a tomboy. I play flag football, swing as high as they do, and I even beat them at board games. I ride down the street on my new Schwinn bike with a red blanket tied around my neck because I feel like Supergirl.

Don't you know? I have power! That blanket flies behind me like a cape, and I know I can do anything, be anything. Remember feeling like that?

I am 10.

My father works two jobs, and today, my mom whispers a familiar phrase, "Wait till your father gets home." When I hear the 55 Chevy drive up and the door slam, we all scatter because we know Dad will grab that handmade leather whip. That was for the four of us. But for me, there was something special.

I am 12.

I am swimming in the pool, and no one is home except Dad and me. When I finish drying off, I head for my room when he stops me and says, "Take off your bathing suit and get into bed with me." I tremble because I do not want another whipping with that homemade leather strap. I do as I am told. As I lay there next to my naked father, I am scared to speak up, petrified to question him and share what I am feeling. I think to myself, *This isn't right. I know Daddy loves me, but this feels wrong.*

After several minutes, I find the courage, and I take my dad's face in my small hands, look right into his eyes, and say, "Daddy, I don't like this."

His face drops, and he replies, "Get up!" A mix of disappointment, shame, and pain in his voice.

Today was the first day I lost that red cape and the beginning of years of losing security and trust.

Later that same year, my father approached me again, and the attacks began. He would sneak into my room after everyone was asleep, Mom knocked out cold on tranquilizing pills. She struggled with manic depression and lost herself early on, and was not there for me. She chose the path of a perpetual victim, feeling utterly helpless, deciding she had zero control over her life. Essentially, despair and hopelessness got the best of her.

The weeks and years that followed the first pool incident, especially after the escalation to that first actual rape in the camper, I struggled to hide the shame and pain. I thought, *How bad am I that my own father is hurting me? He is not treasuring and protecting me? Because that's what should happen..., right?*

I am now 15.

In high school, I was shy and reserved most of the time. I turned to creativity and the arts to express myself because it was a way to be someone else. Performing also affected people, connected to their souls and their hearts, which was difficult for me. Seeing others connect and FEEL something was a happy place for me and helped me connect with them – and to myself, frankly. It was safe for me to feel the pain in a song or portray a character that had an epiphany about what would make their life better. It was exhilarating to be a mirror for possible change.

I am 19.

I can't get out of the house fast enough. And after a secret elopement, an alcoholic husband, and divorce at 21, I feel like a total failure. I pursue a healthcare career that is very lucrative but difficult. My confidence destroyed, I find it hard to speak up with opinions, always worried about judgments, trying to measure up, and feeling like I still fall short.

I am successful – on paper. I still feel empty, depressed, and at times, suicidal. I am not happy. Will I ever get to the other side of this pain? I am continually picking unavailable, manipulative men, which only reinforces my belief that I am not worthy of true love. I feel like I am alone and "on my own," as the *Les Misérables'* song perfectly reflects.

The Turning Point

Today is the day. I am 26.

I'd gone to several counselors but still wasn't feeling any better about my life. Therapy wasn't working. I was determined to overcome the trauma without numbing out on drugs, booze, or medication. I needed support to figure it out. To figure ME out.

So, one chilly evening, I sat in my one-bedroom apartment and listened to my first two-hour taped session with my fourth counselor, whose motto was, "There is no secret to surviving happily. The best way to cope is to live through pain and experience it."

Before I'd reached the end of that first taped session, it hit me like a ton of bricks: almost every answer I'd given him was about me trying to "look" right, trying to prove I was a strong person despite the horrific trauma, and doing just "fine." When I heard myself talking, over and over on those tapes, it was like listening to a defense attorney making a case for how well-adjusted and normal the defendant (me) really was—even after growing up in a crazy, dysfunctional home where my own Father had molested and raped me, repeatedly.

I wanted to show the therapist that I was smarter and far more resilient than most other survivors. *I wasn't honest at all about how I really felt.* I was only playing a role, the superwoman role, and wearing a pretty clever mask to disguise the shame, guilt, anger, and confusion.

This lightning bolt of awareness woke me up: I was *never* going to get a handle on my negative emotions and *never* get a chance to heal—if I couldn't be honest about *all* of it.

The Impact

I was trying to control how others saw me, so I could contain the depths of that pain. Here I was, pretending to be a strong, young woman who'd survived horrific abuse as a child, with barely a scar or internal damage.

But it was a lie.

Back then, appearing "strong" to the rest of the world was more important to me than sharing and healing my deepest pain because asking for help only reinforced my false beliefs that "I'm not good enough," "I'm flawed," and "I'm weak."

I decided to hit the reset button with my counselor and promised to be completely honest with myself and him. Otherwise, there was no way in hell he could help me help myself. I needed to shine a light on those dark fears and negative beliefs driving (and ruining) my life. I needed to become aware of what was really happening under the hood of my psyche.

The Truth Will Set You Free

Believe me, if you're not being honest about what you're feeling and experiencing in life, you're going to keep making decisions based on irrational fears and limiting beliefs that are holding you back. These self-defeating thoughts are psychological roadblocks that stop you from living your own life – they are not reality! They are stories you made up to protect yourself, probably at a young age.

The Ordinary World

From my mother, I learned how the past could grip us by the throat, pull us down with these made-up stories we tell ourselves that keep us small and a victim, the stories that keep us from remembering our power. Yes, dwelling on the past diminishes our true greatness and potential. It slams the door on any future happiness.

That little girl on the bike, wearing a red cape with the "I can do anything! I am great!" attitude was replaced with the "shame and guilt" that comes from sexual abuse. My fathers' powerful mind control and manipulation for a little girl of 12 became hardwired beliefs, affecting my decisions and beliefs for over 30 years.

During those first six intense years, I was so afraid someone would find out about the sexual abuse and how bad I was. And it was up to me to protect the family. I had to control it. It was my responsibility – Dad had said it was.

What were the hardwired beliefs that were born as I protected myself from the pain of abuse?

1. I had to control every situation in my life, or it would fall apart, I would be hurt, or I would not be loved.

2. I had to take responsibility for…everything! Mostly things that went wrong, because if something good happened, it couldn't be due to me.

3. My confidence was shattered, and I could not connect with who I really was, always having to PROVE that I was good at every turn. I was exhausted and never able to reach that place of love, happiness, and fulfillment. Always having to DO MORE – and, to do it perfectly.

I tried to control how others felt about me, prove I'm loveable or that I was enough, avoid judgments, or seek to feel accepted or belong. It's a basic human need to belong, and sometimes we accept situations or say yes when what we really want to say is NO! or run the other direction. This is all at the expense of who we really are and can make us experience strong emotions for abandoning our true selves. This results in sadness, depression, anger, and even feeling more isolated because we are putting on the "I'm okay" mask.

Once I opened my heart to honesty and lost the "I'm okay, I don't need help" mask, and did the work to truthfully connect to my feelings and work through to the *other side of pain*, my life began to change.

Key Lessons and Words of Wisdom

I realize now that the moment I started to release the stories about being unworthy or unlovable, I was free. As soon as I began to love and trust myself, I was free.

I want every woman who has felt stuck or lost or less than, to know she is incredible, and she does have the power to create her life; to remember that what happens to us doesn't define us. It can be the catalyst for change.

Now I speak and teach on how to overcome these barriers to happiness and fulfillment. One tool is my on-line six-week course "Critical Courage - A roadmap to confidence and change." You can access it here:

www.criticalcouragelifemastery.com

My recent books *Shameless* and *The Other Side of Pain* deliver tools for awareness, insights, and change, and what steps to take to find YOU again, leave the past behind, and live for today.

You can check out the books here:

https://criticalcouragebook.com
https://othersideofpain.com

I list below the key lessons I've learned on my journey to fulfillment and love.

Wisdom #1: Honesty is the golden key that unlocks the portal to your true powers and the choices you make.

It ignites your power and potential in your life! If you're *not* honest about *your* feelings and truths, you won't be the one doing the choosing. Instead, your choices will tend to come from a people-pleasing, hollow places. Don't be so busy denying and numbing the past that you're not honest about how it still impacts you today. Only you hold the power to create your own kind of life, the way you like it.

Wisdom #2: I'm free to be 100 percent totally me, my True Self.

Happiness is found when you stop comparing yourself to everyone else and what they want. Stop living for other people and their opinions. Be true to yourself. Don't abandon what you want and need or how you feel. You're the only person in charge of your life.

Wisdom #3: My happiness today is the result of my thoughts.

Happiness starts with you – not your relationships, your job, or your money – but with you. It's not always easy to find happiness within, but it's impossible to find it outside of us.

Wisdom #4: Every experience is just another lesson.

Disappointments and failure are two of the surest stepping stones to success and fulfillment. So, don't let a hard lesson close you down. When things go wrong, learn what you can and then push the tragic thinking and mistakes aside.

Wisdom #5: Nothing changes if nothing changes.

If you don't like your current situation, *do* something about it. There's an old saying, "The definition of crazy is doing the same thing repeatedly and expecting a different result." You have the power of choice to change.

Wisdom #6: It's time for a change when you are feeling stuck.

Overwhelmed and paralyzed, we lose faith and beat ourselves up for not being able to do XYZ. Whenever you're feeling this way, know that it's time to take action to make a change. Any small step will do.

Wisdom #7: What other people think about me is their issue, not mine.

This one was hard. Don't take on other people's negative energy and don't take it personally. What others say and do and their opinions are based entirely on their own self-reflection. So, let that go.

Wisdom #8: Who I spend time with matters

Hang with those who see the greatest potential in you, even when you don't see it in yourself. Spend time with high-vibration people who share your love of life and aren't dragging you down or judging you; we do enough of that ourselves.

Wisdom #9: Even when I'm struggling, there's so much to be grateful for.

Happiness doesn't come from getting something we don't have but appreciating everything we do have. Stress thrives when your worry list grows longer than your gratitude list. Happiness thrives when your gratitude list grows longer than your worry list. So, get your grateful on now.

Wisdom #10: The work to get to *the other side* is worth it.

Life is not easy. There are **no shortcuts to happiness or any place worth going.** Enjoy the journey and the challenge. Know the value in your efforts and *be patient, loving, and kind with yourself.* Realize that patience isn't about waiting; it's about keeping a good attitude while being determined to live your dreams. Know the power of the work; It is well worth it in the end.

The Reward

I am so happy and grateful for the experiences and lessons of my life. It's been an adventure *back for me*, and life is terrific! I have found the love of my life (and a Dr., no less!), and together we feed our souls and creativity singing together in our country band. Check it out at:

www.crystalwhiskey.com

We love to travel with family and friends, and we are looking forward to our second African photo safari in 2022.

I am performing again on stage and in film, and in 2020 I starred in two films, one that garnered over 15 awards at several international film festivals. For my Hollywood-based production company, I have produced and directed several cable TV series, promos, and commercials, including the *Nature Series TV ArtScapes*®

www.tvartscapes.com

Power Summary

So, my dear ones, for review: Any negative past experiences that we have had that make us feel less than, can affect self-worth, confidence, trust, choices, and personal power. It doesn't need to be abuse or trauma. And when those negative, impactful experiences happen in our lives, remembering who we really are, in the moment, can be extremely difficult, especially if there are unconscious stories we are telling ourselves about who we are because of those experiences.

Success Actions

Here are three simple success steps that can help with moving from the pain of the past to freedom and living for today:

- **Awareness.** Take inventory of your feelings. Be honest and do the work to evaluate the stories and judgments you have behind those feelings. If you need additional support, seek it out.

- **Self-Care and Love.** Invest *at least* 10% of your energy in yourself. Set aside "ME" time to develop your "self" and nurture your body and mind. This makes it easier to connect with what you really want for YOU. If you are busy taking care of everyone else or proving you measure up, you might be a major success but are not enjoying the success, not enjoying life, feeling unfulfilled, empty, and always thinking things like, "Is this it?" Always evaluate where YOU are in the picture. You're worth it.

- **Speak Up and Express Your True "I AM."** That is who you really are and who you want to "BE." No excuses or apology. Be daring and place yourself out in the world with opinions, choices, and vulnerability.

Don't let any past define who you are TODAY. Remember that the past does not equal the future, and NOW is the only true time. If you remember this in every circumstance and have faith that Mother/Father/God, the universe, whatever that is for you, will present what is best and next for you on this road called "life." Then you will always have the Critical Courage for the next steps, choices, and change.

Thank you, my friends, family, and mentors who played an enormous part in my growth and success; for guiding me to uncover the genuine gold within and deeper self-awareness and love. You know who you are. Thank you, Mother/Father/God, for connection and the truth about who I really am and how much I have to offer.

Many Blessings, and see you out in the world!

Be Kind. Be Brave. Be Love.

Veronica Crystal Young

About the Author

Veronica Crystal Young brings the perfect combination of experience and education to the table when transforming the lives of unhappy, unfulfilled, and discouraged women trying to get ahead personally and professionally. Aside from all that she brings with her 30-year experience as a corporate healthcare manager, her creative endeavors as a filmmaker, actress, and singer, Veronica also boasts coaching accreditation from Coaches Training Institute and the Forton Group.

NASDAQ, Harvard Club of Boston, Global Society for Female Executives, and Carnegie Hall are just a few of the many notable places and organizations where Veronica has inspired audiences.

Contacts

A resilience expert with Neuro-Linguistic Programming Certification, Veronica shares her abuse and trauma experience and how she refused to let those events define her on her personal website:

www.veronicacrystalyoung.com

Veronica shares her personal stories to help individuals grow in personal resiliency, compassion, hope, and love on stage and in her books. She has authored two books:

- Shameless – 7 Steps to Reclaim your Power The Critical Courage to Change

  https://criticalcouragebook.com

- The Other Side of Pain – Overcoming Childhood Sexual Abuse, recounting how resilience and courage have shaped her future despite a painful past.

  https://othersideofpain.com

Veronica's example is a beacon of hope and light for all women that ever wanted more out of life and felt tethered to the trauma of their past.

Embrace the Unlimited Opportunities

Dr. Veronica Joseph, D.O.M.
Holistic Health Expert, Allergy Specialist, Mentor, and Healer, USA.

*"Visualization is more powerful than knowledge. Dream
the limitless possibilities and Make it Happen!"*
~ Dr. Veronica Joseph, D.O.M.

The Meltdown

*H*ow can I end my life easily? How many sleeping pills can I take, so I do not need to wake up? Why do I have to go through this endless *suffering?* I asked myself. I could not take it any longer, feeling trapped and not seeing a way out of my own misery.

In retrospect, my first labor with my son was difficult. I had a severe, sustained allergic reaction to anesthesia that caused a high fever, dizziness, hallucinations, and extreme fatigue. I could hardly push him out of my belly. Half-awake and half-dreaming, and fortunately, with the encouragement of my gynecologist, the delivery was normal.

With a colicky baby who cried most of the night with itchy skin on both legs and scaly patches on his scalp, I had sleepless nights taking care of him. After a few months, I had abdominal cramps while eating certain foods that caused a loss of appetite. It was overwhelming for me to look after my son, which triggered weakness, sadness, and isolation. After taking antibiotics prescribed for a strep throat diagnosis, his eczema worsened, and he developed hives.

The doctor's recommendations for changing my son's diet by eliminating dairy, wheat, and eggs and applying cortisone cream to his skin did not work. His worsening condition dictated that I make some tough but necessary decisions – I quit my job to take care of him.

Seeing my son suffer so severely even pushed me to the point of suicidal thoughts. I did not know what to do to comfort him nor to relieve myself from worries. As a mother, I felt hopeless, limited, lost, helpless, and utterly alone. My every thought, my every action, was focused on him. It felt like carrying a heavy load of weight on my back (and in my heart) that I could not get rid of.

The Turning Point

As a result of my frustration with the advice and treatments from Western medical doctors, I began to try other alternative therapies. NAET (Nambudripad's Allergy Elimination Techniques) worked for my son and me. NAET can reprogram the brain, reset the nervous system, and remove blockages from nerve pathways to desensitize allergens and return the body to its normal healthy state. NAET protocol is followed by acupressure or acupuncture to reinforce the treatment. After noticing an improvement within one week, I knew that NAET could assist those with similar issues.

For that reason, I went back to school and got my M.S. Degree in Oriental Medicine. To get more clinical training, I worked for a chiropractor and an acupuncturist. In addition, I added Wholistic Kinesiology and NAET certifications to my credentials.

The Impact

After hiring a business coach, I gained greater clarity about how best to create my business vision, mission, and marketing strategy. These newly sharpened ideas allowed me to make several unique programs and specialized services that fully satisfy the needs of my patients.

Today, I take great pride in being able to customize and personalize each patient's plan according to their specific demands. Meeting each patient precisely where they are offers a highly customized and conscientious approach that yields extraordinary results. Also, working with other practitioners prompted me to have monthly virtual workshops.

I have recognized the vital importance of broadening my areas of expertise and widening my capabilities to better serve my patients. These activities include taking classes, investing in new technology that allows clients the opportunity to do online scheduling, designing my own dynamic website, coordinating targeted email campaigns, or constantly modernizing and improving my marketing strategy.

Focusing and learning more about my patients enabled me to provide an excellent customer service that has energized them to overcome their challenges and improve their quality of life.

As a result, my visibility has increased, I receive more new patients from referrals, Internet, workshops, and sponsored groups, and my skills and expertise are being shared with an ever-widening circle of new patients, which to me is the ultimate form of gratification.

Case Studies

I remember one of my patients, Lanie. The first time I saw her, she was crying and was emotionally overwhelmed. Lanie had immune deficiency issues, allergies, asthma, sleep disorder, fatigue, and a digestive disorder. After treating her for a few months, her skin, emotions, digestion, sleep patterns, and energy have all drastically improved. She does yoga, jogs in the morning, and generally feels happier each day. When Lanie referred five new patients to me, the circle of wellness I've been able to create expanded.

Another example was at 3 a.m., after hearing a loud noise in the bathroom at home, I saw my son was lying on the bathroom floor in his own vomit. He could not sit nor stand up. My first thought was that he had food poisoning. So, I immediately performed NAET and acupuncture on him. After removing the needles, he was back to normal as if nothing had happened. He slept through the rest of the night without any problem. I did not have to call an emergency hotline nor take him to the hospital. Feeling confident after I was able to cure my son, all my resilience and sacrifices have paid off!

The Truth Will Set Me Free

The year 2020 has been a difficult year for many. I am grateful I was able to provide online services during the COVID-19 outbreak which started in March 2020. This period taught me to be flexible and not limit myself.

During the first wave of the pandemic, we were in lockdown. So instead of seeing patients in person, I started seeing them virtually, practicing telemedicine. I offered a money-back guarantee if the services did not work out for them.

Case Studies

- For two days, Dana had a fever, cough, nausea, and headaches. Two days after the telemedicine, she was back to normal without any symptoms.

- Elena was experiencing diarrhea and feeling weak. Two days after the telehealth, her diarrhea cleared, but now she had a fever, nasal congestion, difficulty breathing, and was coughing. Two days after the remote treatment, she was feeling better. Her symptoms had disappeared completely.

- Rosa accidentally dialed my phone number and told me that she was experiencing dizziness, nausea, her blood pressure and glucose level had increased, and she had an occipital headache. After treating her remotely, I prayed, trusted, and surrendered to the Higher Power. I told her to call 911 if her condition did not improve. The next day, she informed me that two hours after the remote treatment, her vitals stabilized back to normal, and her symptoms had cleared.

Realizing that knowledge and wisdom are within me, it is essential to trust my intuition, surrender to the universe, and let THY Will be done. Trying to do my best and detaching myself from the outcome are useful. It is also vital to let go of my limiting beliefs, thoughts, and judgments. Being a pure channel of love and light from the Source can assist me to serve humanity. In addition, it is pertinent to have understanding, compassion, empathy, and love for myself and others. Most significantly, I believe in treating my patients as family.

My Origins

It was a blessing to grow up in the Philippines, a beautiful place known for its pristine beaches and delicious cuisine.

My mom was a full-time homemaker taking care of nine children, and my dad worked as a postal clerk in a U.S. Airbase. After working full time, my dad would collect left-over foods from restaurants and bring it home by riding in a "jeepney" (small painted bus), so he could feed the pigs and chickens. He tried his best to be a good provider. The values my parents instilled in us included the importance of family, love of God, hard work, kindness, and generosity.

My brothers moved to the United States to serve in the military. My family followed them. My youngest brother and I immigrated last in 1985 after I completed my B.S. in Computer Science. It was difficult for me to move to a new country and a completely new life. Fortunately, with aid from my family, I gradually began to adjust. I could hardly speak and understand the English language, especially when people spoke so fast. I experienced discrimination when people thought I was stupid because of my heavy accent when I spoke English. To attend college, I took a course in English as a Second Language.

It took me another six years to earn a B.S. in Information Systems

Management at the University of San Francisco while working full-time. This demanded perseverance, hard work, sleepless nights, long walks, and transferring to different buses just to get to school. At one point, I was assaulted the night before my final exam while walking alone. Despite these hurdles, I persisted and finally graduated! I was the first person in our family to graduate from an American college!

The Main Lessons and Words of Wisdom

When my son and I had physical issues, it led me to my true calling of assisting others with their illness. I became an entrepreneur to build my own practice. In addition, all the obstacles I faced and conquered gave me strength, empathy, courage, resilience, and compassion, all of which allows me to better relate to and connect with my patients. I know how they feel because I have been there.

I help women heal their allergies, immune system dysfunction, and digestive issues by resolving the root cause of their symptoms while empowering them with self-care tools so they can enhance their well-being and fully enjoy their lives.

My mission is to elevate their consciousness by knowing their Divine Truth. We are all Divine beings who are infinite and unlimited, trying to co-create with Source according to the Divine Plan and manifest it in the physical realm here on Earth.

Below is the list of lessons I have learned that will hopefully inspire, encourage, and motivate you to make your own dreams come true!

1. Unconditional Love

Pure love is the most powerful healing energy. It is true giving without expectations and attachments. It vibrates at a very high frequency. Release all judgments that do not serve your higher purpose. Put yourself in other people's shoes so you can understand them more fully. Have sympathy with yourself and others. Healing starts with forgiveness. It releases all toxins and poisons in your body. It also opens and heals your heart.

Affirm every day:

"Divine love is flowing and restoring every cell and organs of my body. Pure love is the magnet that captivates the right people and things towards me. I am peace. I am love. I am joy."

2. Design Your Life

Create your own blueprint. How do you want to live your life? Make an album of photographs that you want to unfold in your life. Imagine your best day – see, taste, and feel it is happening every day. Make a roadmap of how to get there. Be resourceful. Research, hire a mentor, educate, and reinvent yourself. Put your master plan into action and make it happen!

"Victory is a compilation of inspiration, preparation, hard work, learning from failures, and resilience."

3. Count Your Blessings each Day

There is no such thing as "bad luck." Whatever you put out to the universe comes back to you.

Reflect on your difficulties as gifts, blessings, and opportunities to learn so you can grow and evolve. Be grateful for any experiences you have – good or bad.

"No poison can kill a positive thinker, and no medicine can save a negative thinker."
~ Buddha

4. Recharge Your Battery

What is your priority in life? Work smart by managing your time. You cannot sustain others effectively if you are drained and depleted. Have a spiritual routine to nourish your body, mind, and spirit. It can include exercise, Tai Chi Chih, meditation, prayer, and spending time with nature, family, friends, and other support groups. Maintain a balanced lifestyle.

"A healthy body has a wealthy mind. It is cheaper and easier to prevent a disease than to treat it."

5. Do What You Love

You can be resilient if you are passionate about your work. Do not be afraid to fail. Learn the lessons from your mistakes, refine or change your strategy, and keep expanding. Everything changes with the passage of time, so be flexible, committed, and relentless until you succeed. Be unconventional and think outside of the norm.

> *"Success is not the key to happiness; happiness is the key to success. If you love what you're doing, you will be successful."*
> ~ Albert Schweitzer

6. Surrender

Surrender is not giving up. It is letting go of limiting beliefs and thoughts instilled in us by our family and society. Imagine the endless positive outcomes. We are infinite beings. It is our Divine heritage. Everything is possible. What are the thoughts and beliefs that are empowering and disempowering you? How do they affect you physically, mentally, emotionally, and spiritually?

Beliefs and thoughts can form our lives and can become our own reality. Aligning our ego-mind to our higher-mind through meditation can overcome any hardship in life.

Affirm:
> *"As a Divine being, my will power is greater than my adversities. I apply my creative intelligence to solve any problems."*

7. Be Mindful

Be present and enjoy each moment. Act as an observer and try not to become too deeply involved in emotional entanglements. At the end of the day, reflect on your experiences. What have you learned? What emotions did you feel? E-motion is energy-in-motion responding to situations. Be kind to yourself. Acknowledge your mistakes and negative reactions. What triggered them? Embrace the gifts and lessons learned.

> *"Don't wait to be successful at some future point. Have a successful relationship with the present moment and be fully present in whatever you are doing. That is success."*

~ Eckhart Tolle

8. "Soul" Purpose

What is your soul's purpose? What is your legacy? Make a difference. Reach out to others in need. Create a product or service that is in alignment with your higher purpose. How can it enrich others? Build it around your customers. Have the courage to take risks.

"The universe isolates you so you can find your soul's purpose. It may seem like you've lost friendships and relationships, but finding your path, passion, and purpose in life is worth more!
For where your soul is, there you will find your treasure."
~ The Minds Journal

The REWARD

I am thankful that my online business and services are expanding. In addition to in-person consultation and treatment, I do online workshops, provide remote services such as universal rays healing, nutritional consultation, and telehealth. I have more freedom, aid people anywhere in the world, and spend more time with my family. My work is not tied to one location. Best of all, I can help my family with their health conditions as well as my own, which is priceless for me!

When you surrender and release limiting beliefs and thoughts, the possibilities are endless. You can reach your greatest capacity. You can materialize your dreams thru preparation, creativity, diligence, and learning from your mistakes. Have faith and believe in yourself.

When you align your will to the Divine Will, you will experience synchronicity and will see amazing results. You will be more peaceful, harmonious, and joyful in our busy world.

Major Points

1. Fill in the blank. Beliefs and thoughts can _____.
2. What were the lessons I learned during the first Covid-19 outbreak?
3. How can I let go of limiting beliefs and thoughts?

Key Actions

Below are three crucial steps that can further actualize your own dream:

1. Accept and love yourself. Write down the qualities that you like about yourself, including the accomplishments and challenges you overcame. Put these in a cookie jar. When you are experiencing self-doubt or anxiety, pull out a paper you have written from the cookie jar to make yourself feel better. Then admit and recognize your insecurities and fears. Why are you afraid? Release those self-judgments and attachments to principles that are not benefiting you.

2. Practice self-discipline. Meditate for at least 30 minutes regularly. Do Qi Gong, Tai Chi Chih, or yoga. These routines can guide you to align with your Higher Self, allowing you to access your advanced inner wisdom. Be receptive. Open your heart and mind to new ideas, things, people, and places.

3. Begin keeping a spiritual diary. At the end of each day, write at least three things that you are grateful for. Give thanks. What have you learned? What could have you done better? Keep improving. Give yourself the permission to receive. The more you receive from the universe, the more you can give.

I am including you in my prayers, blessing you with Divine Love and Light, and wishing you the best!

> "Dream the impossible and let go of your limiting beliefs.
> By the Law of Attraction, you can achieve what you believe."

Blessings and love,

Veronica

About the Author

Dr. Veronica Joseph, D.O.M., earned her Master of Science Degree in Oriental Medicine at Southwest Acupuncture College in Albuquerque, New Mexico. She is a certified Diplomate in Oriental Medicine by NCCAOM (National Certification Commission for Acupuncture and Oriental Medicine), a licensed Doctor of Oriental Medicine in New Mexico, and a licensed Acupuncturist in California.

She is also a certified NAET (Nambudripad's Allergy Elimination Techniques) Practitioner, certified in Wholistic Kinesiology, Universal Rays Healing Level 1, 2, 3, Seven Rays Master, and a Reiki Master. Her specialties include allergies, digestive issues, immune system dysfunction, and pain management. Her goal is to educate and empower her patients to achieve optimum health and reach their highest potential.

Contacts

Schedule a FREE Optimum Wellness Session.
Email: mail to: vernonica@awesomehealing.com
During our phone consultation, we will discuss your health goals, challenges, and recommendations to:

- Improve your Digestion

- Alleviate Food Allergies

- Enhance your immune system

- Boost your Energy

- Relieve Pain

Download a FREE Guide "9 Keys to Overcome Food Allergies"
Website: https://www.awesomehealing.com

Join our Facebook Group: Wholistic Healing to Overcome Allergies
https://www.facebook.com/groups/362911764396085/

Like our Facebook Page
https://www.facebook.com/Awesome-Healing-Acupuncture-376192685732695/

Register for our monthly online Health and Wellness Workshop
https://www.awesomehealing.com/workshop-dup

LinkedIn: https://www.linkedIn.com/veronica-joseph-a98531a9/